Corns and Bartleet

The Birmingham Riots of 1791

Corns and Bartleet

The Birmingham Riots of 1791

ISBN/EAN: 9783337251536

Printed in Europe, USA, Canada, Australia, Japan

Cover: Foto ©ninafisch / pixelio.de

More available books at **www.hansebooks.com**

THE
BIRMINGHAM RIOTS

OF

1791:

A CLOSELY COPIED REPRINT OF A PAMPHLET PUBLISHED IMMEDIATELY AFTER THEIR OCCURRENCE.

WITH AN INTRODUCTION.

BIRMINGHAM:
CORNS & BARTLEET, UNION STREET.
SOLD BY HAMILTON, ADAMS, AND CO., PATERNOSTER ROW, LONDON.
1867.

PRICE ONE SHILLING.

Birmingham:
Corns and Bartleet, Printers,
Union Street.

INTRODUCTION.

IT happened some thirty years ago that a party of learned geologists, who had been hammering among the fells of Cumberland and Westmoreland, in out of the way districts, during a fortnight, came on a Saturday evening into the inn at Buttermere, and, while their dinner was preparing, asked for a newspaper to while away the interval: "Any old paper will do, landlord," said Dr. WHEWELL, "for myself and Professors AIRY and BUCKLAND have not seen one for nearly three weeks." "Here, sir," rejoined the landlord, "is an account of the French Revolution." "The French Revolution!" exclaimed Dr. BUCKLAND "come, landlord, we asked for an old newspaper, but not one quite so old as that." "Oh, sir," says the landlord, "it was only down here yesterday and the Revolution happened the day before." The learned *savans* had thought of the Revolution of 1830, and that nothing like it could happen afterwards; the newspaper told them of the flight of Charles X, and the Bourbons driven from the throne.

That History but repeats itself is an aphorism whose truth may be recognized in the fact that, while this reprint (in the original old fashioned type and text, having no other object than the preservation of a valuable record of local history of "an "authentic Account of the Riots of Birmingham of "the 14th, 15th, 16th, and 17th days of July, "1791,") was passing through the press, more riots of another July, in 1867, have been occurring in our town, and that, as before, "at this period the civil "power was found insufficient to restore peace, and it "became necessary to apply to Government for "military aid, granted with an alacrity that claims the "gratitude of the inhabitants," rendering it necessary once more again, after a lapse of nearly three quarters of a century "to inform the stranger, that "the manufacturers, and labouring class of people, in "this town, are brought up in the earliest habits of "industry; that at five or six years of age they "become useful in the manufactories, in which chil- "dren of both sexes are usually placed; and that the "attention which their employments require, together "with the necessary relaxation from business, leave "little or no time for the improvement of the mind :— "they are taught to *act*, and not to *think*."

The following pages are printed *fac simile* to the pamphlet alluded to, the quaintness of style and orthography being strictly observed.

S. C.

RAVENHURST STREET, BIRMINGHAM,
    September 26, 1867.

AN
AUTHENTIC ACCOUNT
OF

The Riots in Birmingham,

On the 14th, 15th, 16th, and 17th Days of July, 1791;

ALSO,

The JUDGE's CHARGE, the PLEADINGS of the COUNSEL,
AND THE SUBSTANCE OF THE EVIDENCE GIVEN ON

The Trials of the Rioters.

AND

AN IMPARTIAL COLLECTION OF

LETTERS, &c.

Written by the Supporters of the Eftablifhment and the Diffenters,
in confequence of the Tumults.

THE WHOLE COMPILED,

In order to preferve to Pofterity the genuine Particulars and Connexions
of an Event, which

ATTRACTED THE ATTENTION OF EUROPE.

PRINTED (FOR THE COMPILER) AND

SOLD BY J. BELCHER, IN DERITEND;

Sold alfo by T. PEARSON, and T. WOOD, High-ftreet; the other
Bookfellers in Birmingham;

AND BY J. JOHNSON, ST. PAUL'S CHURCH-YARD, LONDON.

Price One Shilling.

CONTENTS.

	Page
The PREFACE, stating the origin of the tumults	ix.
Advertisement for the commemoration dinner	1
The inflammatory hand-bill	2
Incendiary refuted, in reply to ditto	ibid
Advertisement for the author, &c. of the hand-bill	3
Advertisement from the Revolutionists	ibid
Account of the RIOTS	4
The thanks of the Dissenters to those who protected their property	11
Notice to receive informations	ibid
Trials of the Rioters	12
Two addresses to his Majesty	22
Dr. Priestley's letter to the inhabitants of Birmingham	24
Letter from Mr. Keir	26
Mr. Keir's second letter, with the Toasts	28
Lover of Truth, to Dr. Priestley and Mr. Russell	33
John Churchman, to Dr. Priestley	37
An Inhabitant, to ditto	39
Clericus, to ditto	41
Dr. Priestley to the Printer of the Birm. Gazette	42

Advertise-

CONTENTS.

	Page
Advertisement from the Dissenters' Committee	42
Three advertisements connected with the Riots	43, 44
Dr. Tatham to the Dissenters	45
Address of George Rous, Esq.	50
Letter from the Morning Chronicle	51
Extract from the Preface to the Rev. Mr. Scholefield's Sermon	56
Letter from M. Condorcet to Dr. Priestley	58
Dr. Priestley's answer	59
Address from the Society at the Jacobins to Dr. Priestley	60
From the Revolution Society to Dr. Priestley	61
Declaration of the Belfast Volunteers	63
Address and Declaration from the Thatched-house Tavern	65

THE PREFACE.

IN delineating the rise and progress of the late alarming Riots in Birmingham, it will be the aim of the compiler to relate facts, simple and unadorned—plain truth he prefers to flowery fiction; and no consideration shall induce him to relate a circumstance, or hazard an assertion, which he has not the most convincing reason to believe strictly just.

The depredations committed, were of such a nature as to attract the attention of all Europe; and it must be matter of enquiry, among thinking people, what could possibly induce, or stimulate, the once peaceable inhabitants of Birmingham (remarked for their industry and obedience to the laws) to such atrocious and daring acts of violence?

It may not be improper to inform the stranger, that the manufacturers, and labouring class of people, in this town, are brought up in the earliest habits of industry; that at five or six years of age they become useful in the manufactories, in which children of both sexes are usually placed; and that the attention which their employments require, together with the necessary relaxations from business, leave little or no time for the improvement of the mind:—they are taught to act, *and not to* think.

THE PREFACE.

The late vigorous and repeated attempts of the Dissenters to obtain a repeal of the Corporation and Test Laws, excited much alarm and apprehension amongst many of the established Clergy, and was most forcibly felt by those residing in Birmingham. The name and writings of Dr. Priestley *are as much dreaded by his opponents, as they are admired by his friends; and as he long resided near this town, and was eminently conspicuous in his endeavours to procure a Repeal of those Acts, it is not surprising that his sentiments should be represented to the lower classes of the people as* dangerous *to the Church and State.*

Attacks made upon his principles and motives in different pulpits were answered from the press, which produced his "Familiar Letters to the Inhabitants of Birmingham." *In these letters his opponents are treated with irony, and his candid readers convinced by a train of reasoning, bold, conclusive, and irresistible. But as the Doctor had asserted, that* "would not insure the ecclesiastical establishment of this country for twenty years," *and that* "he was laying grains of gunpowder, which would blow up the fabric;" *the* mischievous thinkers *found no difficulty in persuading the* unthinking actors, *that he meant literally what he had asserted—and strange as it may appear, yet it is strictly true, that many thought it was the real intention of the Dissenters* to Destroy the Churches!—*Whereas it would be an insult to common sense to suppose the Doctor meant otherwise, than the*
sunshine

THE PREFACE.

sunshine of reason would assuredly chase away and dissipate the mists of darkness and error, and when the people felt *themselves oppressed by any* set of men, THEY *had the power to redress the grievance.*

The minds of the inferior classes being thus prejudiced and contaminated, an opportunity *was only wanting to shew their* attachment *to the* Church and King; *this opportunity presented itself upon notice being given, that it was the intention of the friends of freedom to celebrate the Anniversary of the French Revolution. (The invitation for this purpose, with the papers written in consequence of it, appear in proper order.)* So animated with religion and loyalty *were these partizans, that it is more than probable the subsequent devastations would have taken place, if the Friends of the Revolution had not assembled; for they had separated some hours before the attack upon the Hotel windows.*

As a further stimulus to the exertions of the populace, a report was industriously circulated amongst them, that the Magistrates were unfriendly to the Dissenters, and would protect *them in the destruction of their places of worship. The assertion was sufficient to gain implicit credit with the people I have described, and thus,* armed with authority, *it was the work of* duty *as well as of* choice; *for they have long looked upon the Magistrates as the sole sources of knowledge and legal information.* Unfortunately, *it was not till after inebriation and success had rendered* them ungovernable, *that* active measures *were employed to undeceive them.*

At

At this period the civil power was found insufficient to restore peace, and it became necessary to apply to Government for military aid; it was granted with an alacrity that claims the gratitude of the inhabitants of Birmingham—and the rapid march of three troops of Light Horse to our relief, exhilirated the spirits of every peaceable individual, and contributed to the dispersion of the banditti. As an acknowledgment for the expedition and good behaviour of these troops, the Dissenters, on the re-establishment of order, presented *them with One Hundred Pounds;* and at a Town's Meeting the like sum was voted to the privates; also a handsome sword to each officer—and a piece of plate, value One Hundred Guineas, to each of the Magistrates.

To the Noblemen and Gentlemen who attended, in order to restore the public tranquility, the utmost praise is due; and their names and exertions will long be revered and admired, by the late suffering and desponding inhabitants of this large and opulent town.

Birmingham, Sept. 26, 1791.

AN ACCOUNT

OF THE

RIOTS, &c.

IN the Preface to this work we have endeavoured to state, with truth and impartiality, the grounds of animosity subsisting between the supporters of the establishment, and the dissenters; we now proceed to relate the circumstances connected with this business, previous to the late alarming riots. The first advertisement, announcing the intentions of the Friends of Freedom, was as follows:—

"*Hotel, Birmingham, July* 7, 1791.

"Commemoration of the French Revolution.

"A number of gentlemen intend dining together on the 14th instant, to commemorate the auspicious day which witnessed the emancipation of twenty-six millions of people from the yoke of despotism, and restored the blessings of equal government to a truly great and enlightened nation; with whom it is our interest, as a commercial people, and our duty, as friends to the general rights of mankind, to promote a free intercourse, as subservient to a permanent friendship.

"Any Friend to Freedom, disposed to join the intended temperate festivity, is desired to leave his name at the bar of the Hotel, where tickets may be had at Five Shillings each, including a bottle of wine; but no person will be admitted without one.

"Dinner will be on table at three o'clock precisely."

On the second appearance of this advertisement, in the Birmingham Gazette, the following was likewise inserted:

"*On Friday next will be published, price One Halfpenny,*

"An authentic list of all those who dine at the Hotel, Temple Row, Birmingham, on Thursday the 14th instant, in commemoration of the French Revolution.

"*Vivant Rex et Regina.*"

This last advertisement was certainly intended to intimidate the meeting at the Hotel and alarm the people. The author was successful in his plan, and may congratulate himself on the consequences of it;—but about this time a few copies of the following imprudent and seditious hand-bill were privately circulated, and increased the growing ferment:

"*My Countrymen,*

"THE second year of Gallic Liberty is nearly expired. At the commencement of the third, on the 14th of this month, it is devoutly to be wished, that every enemy to civil and religious despotism, would give his sanction to the *majestic common cause,* by a public celebration of the anniversary. Remember that on the 14th of July the Bastile, that " High Altar and Castle of Despotism" fell. Remember the enthusiasm, *peculiar* to the cause of Liberty, with which it was attacked. Remember that generous humanity that taught the oppressed, groaning under the weight of insulted rights, to save the lives of oppressors! Extinguish the mean prejudices of nations; and let your numbers be collected, and sent as a free-will offering to the National Assembly.

" But is it possible to forget that your own Parliament is venal? Your Minister hypocritical? Your Clergy legal oppressors? The Reigning Family extravagant? The Crown of a certain Great Personage becoming every day too weighty for the Head that wears it? Too weighty for the People who *gave* it? Your Taxes partial and excessive? Your Representation a cruel *insult* upon the sacred rights of Property, Religion, and Freedom?

" But on the 14th of this month, prove to the political sycophants of the day, that You reverence the Olive Branch; that You *will* sacrifice to public Tranquility, till the Majority *shall* exclaim, *The Peace of Slavery is worse than the War of Freedom.* Of that moment let Tyrants beware."

This paper was immediately succeeded by the following:

"*An Incendiary Refuted.*

"A Paper having been distributed in the town this morning, evidently calculated to weaken the attachment of the people to the present excellent form of government, and to excite tumults similar to those which have produced the most atrocious murders, anarchy, and distress in a neighbouring kingdom :—it is thought proper to apprize the good and peaceable subjects of this place, that *every position* in that seditious hand-bill, is *false* and *factious* as the *wretch* who composed it.

"The perfect enjoyment we now experience, of every blessing, freedom, and protection a mild government can bestow, is the best

refutation

refutation of the detestable calumnies of the author of the hand-bill; and whatever the *modern republicans* may imagine, or the *regicidical propounders of the rights of men* design, let us convince them there is enough of loyalty in the majority of the inhabitants of this country to *support* and *defend* their King; and that we are not so destitute of common sense, as not to prefer the *order, liberty, happiness,* and *wealth,* which is diffused through every portion of the British Empire —to the *anarchy,* the *licentiousness,* the *poverty,* and the *misery* which now overwhelm the degraded kingdom of France.

"*Birmingham, Monday, July* 11, 1791."

Many copies of the inflammatory hand-bill were taken, and read with avidity; but the Magistrates (Joseph Carles, Esq., and the Rev. Dr. Spencer) in conjunction with the High Bailiff, and nine other gentlemen, in order to show their detestation of such publications, caused the following advertisement to be inserted in the Birmingham and Stafford Chronicle on Thursday (the day of the meeting) :—

"ONE HUNDRED GUINEAS REWARD.

"*Birmingham, July* 13, 1791.

" Whereas a certain seditious and criminal hand-bill, intending to inflame the minds of the people against Government, was circulated in this town on Monday last, a reward of One Hundred Guineas is hereby offered to any person who will discover either the writer, printer, publisher, or distributer, so that he or they may be convicted thereof."

And the gentlemen who proposed meeting at the Hotel, also caused the following to be inserted in the same paper:

"*Birmingham Commemoration of the French Revolution.*

"Several hand-bills having been circulated in the town, which can only be intended to create distrust concerning the intention of the meeting, to disturb its harmony, and inflame the minds of the people; the gentlemen who proposed it, think it necessary to declare their entire disapprobation of all such hand-bills, and their ignorance of the authors.

"Sensible themselves of the advantages of a Free Government, they rejoice in the extension of Liberty to their Neighbours; at the same time avowing, in the most explicit manner, their *firm attachment* to the *Constitution of their own Country,* as vested in the Three Estates of *King, Lords,* and *Commons.* Surely no Free-born Englishman can refrain from exulting in this addition to the general mass of

human

human happiness? It is the Cause of Humanity! It is the Cause of the People!

"*Birmingham, July* 13, 1791."

Whether the inflammatory hand-bill was written by an imprudent Friend of the Revolution, or an enemy to the Dissenters, is not known at present; certain it is, that every attempt to trace it to its source has hitherto proved ineffectual, notwithstanding the Dissenters have since offered an additional reward of One Hundred Guineas, and Government (in order to discountenance such publications, and sanction the zealous efforts of its friends in Birmingham) have also proclaimed a further reward of One Hundred Pounds.—The criminality of this bill appears chiefly to consist in its publication at such a period, as (if it was not the intention of the author) it was natural to conclude that it might produce improper effects, irritated as the populace already were, and to which the large reward offered for the Publisher, on the day of festivity, might perhaps a little contribute. With respect to the matter it contains (however indecent and untrue it may be found) it is not more virulent than "Paine's Rights of Man," "Mackintosh's Answer to Burke," " Remarks on the Constitution of England," &c., &c., which have been lately published without incurring the censure of Government.——We now proceed to the Commemoration; and from the conduct and declarations of the gentlemen who composed the meeting, the most prejudiced cannot surely assert that there appeared the *least tendency on their part* to promote anarchy and confusion; on the contrary, they acted as became the free subjects of a free state, not only enjoying the blessings of their own government, but rejoicing that a neighbouring nation, like themselves, could sit down unshackled and unoppressed by Tyranny and Despotism.

On Thursday the 14th of July, 1791, in conformity to their advertisement, eighty-one gentlemen assembled at the Hotel, in Temple-row, to commemorate the Anniversary of the French Revolution; many persons were assembled in front of the house, who expressed the violence of their temper and indecency of their behaviour, by hissing and hustling the gentlemen as they entered. Dinner was served up at three o'clock, and after several toasts had been drank, the company, upon the motion of William Russell, Esq., separated, and departed from the house between five and six. The short time they were together was spent in the most agreeable manner, and they departed thus early in expectation that the populace would

not

not re-assemble. In this idea they were mistaken, for about eight o'clock a large and riotous number had again collected, and notwithstanding the attendance of the magistrates, and the conviction that the company had departed, they demolished the windows in the front of the tavern.

From thence they proceeded to the New Meeting-house (Dr. Priestley's), a large and handsome building, the gates and doors of which were soon burst open, the pews were demolished, the cushions and fragments carried out and burnt in the front of the building, and at length fire was carried in, which consumed it to the outer walls. A very valuable library, belonging to the congregation, was likewise destroyed. Happily for the surrounding neighbours the evening was remarkably serene, or the violence of the flames would have carried certain destruction to a considerable distance.

Soon after the New Meeting-house was forced open, the Old Meeting was attacked by another party, armed with iron crows, bludgeons, &c., who tore down the pulpit, pews, and galleries, and burnt them in the burying-ground; they afterwards set fire to the body of the Meeting, but permitted the engines to play upon the adjoining buildings. The distress of the neighbourhood was great indeed; but by the falling of the roof, and the outer walls, their apprehensions from the conflagration were gradually abated. At the destruction of these, as well as the succeeding places, the rioters were particularly active in securing lead, iron, and various other articles, which they seemed to think themselves fully entitled to for their zeal and industry.

From the Meetings detachments moved off to Dr. Priestley's, at Fair-hill, rather more than a mile from Birmingham, which was attacked with savage fury. They began by breaking down the doors and windows, and throwing from every part of the house the furniture, library, &c. but as some of the Doctor's friends were in the house before the banditti, they employed themselves in packing up and removing part of the library, and several valuable articles of furniture; —unfortunately the books were afterwards discovered, and destroyed. The depredators expressed their disappointment at the Doctor's escape, by the most violent words; and could they have gained possession of his person, the consequences must certainly have proved fatal to him. Happily he was prevailed upon to leave his house before the arrival of the mob, but he had not time to secure any of his manuscripts, the destruction of which he greatly laments, as they were the result of the laborious study of many years, and which he shall never be able to re-compose.

The shrubs, trees, &c., in the garden were torn up, or trampled upon; but there was reason for some time to hope that the Elaboratory (a little distance from the house) would have been saved, nor did it appear to have been noticed as long as the liquors in the cellar lasted, of the spirituous part of which some of the rioters had drank so immoderately, that they seemed no longer to have existence; while others had been rendered so extremely quarrelsome, by the plentiful draughts they had taken of wine and ale, that many battles among themselves were being fought at one time in the adjoining field. The battles collected the greater part of the rioters round them, and the house (the floors of which were now strewed over with torn manuscripts, books, &c.) was, as long as they lasted, almost cleared of them; when, however, they were over, the mob returned to the premises—the Elaboratory was then broken into, the most truly valuable and useful apparatus of philosophical instruments, that (according to the Doctor's declaration) perhaps any individual in this, or in any other country, was ever possessed of, was destroyed. The whole building was soon after set on fire; a man was killed by the falling of a cornice stone, and nothing of the house, offices, &c., now remains but the bare walls.

On Friday morning, as they recovered from the fatigue and intoxication of the preceding night, different parties of the rioters entered the town, to the great consternation of the inhabitants. The doors of every place of confinement were thrown open, and they paraded through the streets armed with bludgeons, loudly vociferating CHURCH AND KING, words which all the inhabitants now chalked upon their window shutters and doors, for the security of their dwellings. In the course cf the morning, the Earl of Aylesford (to whose indefatigable attention and exertions the town has been highly indebted at this alarming season) arrived at Dr. Priestley's; he harangued what remained of the mob at Fair-hill, and brought them from this scene of devastation into the town, where he again addressed them, and persuaded them to disperse, and retire to their respective homes and occupations. About the same time the magistrates of the place, and many of the principal inhabitants were with other parties in the New Church-yard, endeavouring by the most conciliating language to induce them to separate, and desist from further violence. All attempts, however, to check their proceedings, and restore peace and order, proved fruitless.

About two o'clock the elegant mansion of Mr. John Ryland (late Mr. Baskerville's) at Easy-hill, was attacked, and though the rioters were once or twice repulsed, it was not long before they possessed themselves of the house, and set it on fire. Here many of them were so insensible of their danger, that the flames caught them in the upper chambers, and others were in such a state of intoxication, that they could not be drawn from, but perished in, the cellars. Several of the rioters, most terribly scorched and bruised, were conveyed to the Hospital, some of whom are since dead; seven bodies, so much disfigured that they could hardly be recognized, have been dug out of the ruins; and a man on the following Monday (who had been immured in one of the vaults) worked his way out, but soon after expired upon the grass.

While the house of Mr. Ryland was burning, the Magistrates, anxious to preserve the town from further outrage, until the military could arrive, adopted the measure of swearing in a number of the inhabitants as additional Constables. A party of them immediately proceeded to Mr. Ryland's, but after a conflict of some continuance, they were driven off by the enraged multitude, and obliged to retire without effecting any useful purpose.

Information being received about the same time that the country residence of John Taylor, Esq., at Bordesley (about half a mile from the town) was attacked, another party of the gentlemen who had been sworn constables, headed by Captain Carver, repaired thither; they found the rioters in the cellars, and drove them from the premises, of which they kept possession a sufficient length of time to remove Mr. Taylor's title deeds, writings, &c., and some small part of the furniture. Towards the evening, however, by the junction of those from Mr. Ryland's, and other parts, the rioters had acquired such an accession of strength, that all resistance here was ineffectual, and many of the gentlemen were much beaten. Under these circumstances Capt. Carver made a last effort to save the house. He offered the rioters the immediate payment of one hundred guineas if they would not burn it: He was answered by the cry of "No Bribery," hustled immediately into the midst of them, and narrowly escaped their fury. When the night set in, the flames appeared through the roof, and this beautiful and spacious mansion, with most of its superb furniture, stables, offices, and ricks, is reduced to its mere walls.

This night the house of Mr. Hutton, in the High-street, which had been assaulted once or twice in the day, was entered, and com-

pletely

pletely stript of its contents; his large stock of paper, his son's very valuable library, and all his furniture, were destroyed or carried away. A woman made an attempt to fire the house, but was prevented by the surrounding spectators, out of regard to the neighbouring buildings.

From Mr. Hutton's house in town, they proceeded early on Saturday morning to his country house at Washwood Heath, three miles from hence, which, with its offices, they reduced to ashes. The occasion of Mr. Hutton's being so obnoxious to the rioters did not arise from his religious principles, but on account of his being a very active Commissioner of the Court of Requests, in which department he has rendered most essential service to the town.

This morning also, the large and elegant mansion of Mr. George Humphreys, at Spark-brook, was attacked; and from the generosity of Mr. Humphreys, and the remonstrances of his friends, there was reason, for some time, to expect they would have been diverted from their object; but, at length, stupified by intoxication, deaf to remonstrance, and divested of every sentiment of gratitude, they forcibly entered the house (after a smart resistance) and ransacked it of all its rich furniture; after destroying the inside work, breaking all the windows, and doing other mischief, they went off without burning it.

They then proceeded to the house of William Russell, Esq., at Showell-green (the greater part of the furniture of which had been previously removed) and after ransacking it, they consumed it, together with the out-offices.

Mr. T. Hawkes, of Moseley Wake Green, was the next sufferer; his house was stript of its windows, books, and furniture, which were either destroyed, or carried away.

The next object of the rioters was Moseley-Hall, the property of John Taylor, Esq., but occupied by the Dowager Countess of Carhampton, to whom they had given notice to remove her effects; her Ladyship complied with their request, and in the evening this large and beautiful stone mansion, together with all the out-offices, hay ricks, &c., was destroyed.

The house of Mr. Harwood, in the neighbourhood of Moseley, was also burnt and destroyed; as was likewise the house of the Rev. Mr. Hobson, on the Moseley Road.

The terror and distress which pervaded the whole town on Saturday, while these dreadful scenes were acting, will be better conceived than described. The magistrates had tried every means

of

of persuasion, to no effect; large bills were stuck up, requesting all persons to retire to their respective homes, to no purpose; nothing certain was known respecting the approach of the military; and numbers of the rioters, joined by thieves, and drunken prostitutes from every quarter, were, with blue cockades in their hats, in all parts of the town, and in small bodies, levying contributions on the inhabitants. There was scarcely an house-keeper that dared refuse them meat, drink, money, or whatever they demanded. The shops were mostly shut up, business nearly at a stand, and every body employed in secreting and removing their valuables. Very happily, however, the body of the rioters, overcome with liquor and fatigue, lay all the night in the fields, round their conflagrations in the country, and did not come into the town; the first intelligence that was received of them on Sunday morning was, that a party was gone to Kingswood, about seven miles off, where they burnt the Dissenting Meeting-house, and the dwelling-house for the Minister; also the premises of Mr. Cox, a farmer, at Worstock.

In the afternoon accounts were also received that another party had assembled at Edgbaston-hall, the residence of Dr. Withering, which place they visited the day before, but left uninjured, after being regaled with the Doctor's liquor. They now, however, notwithstanding the plentiful manner in which the liquor was dealt out to them, appeared determined to plunder the Hall; some of the rooms were pillaged, and they were even preparing, it is thought, to destroy the place, when information was received that troops were approaching Birmingham. No sooner had the rioters notice of this, than the major part of them sneaked off in different directions, in bodies of ten, twelve, or more together; and the few that at last remained were quickly driven off the premises by the neighbours. Dr. Withering's books, philosophical apparatus, and valuable collections in natural history, suffered much by the hasty removal of them, after his first alarm.

The reader will easily judge what a relief this certain intelligence of the approach of the military must have afforded the alarmed and agitated minds of the inhabitants of the town.—Thousands went out to meet them, and about ten o'clock three troops of the 15th regiment of dragoons, attended by the magistrates, entered this place, amidst the acclamations of the people, and illuminations of the streets through which they passed. They halted at the Swan Inn, where the fatigued and fainting state of both officers and men evinced the exertions they had made for our relief. About seven o'clock that morning the Minister's express had arrived with orders for them to march hither: at half-past ten o'clock they left Nottingham, and though the greater part of their horses were hastily fetched from grass, such was their zeal in the service, that they arrived at Erdington, within four miles of the town (after a journey of upwards of fifty-three miles) a little after seven o'clock.—Captain Polhill, who commanded, brought the troops the first forty miles without halting.

The arrival of the military not only dissipated the apprehensions of the inhabitants, but immediately restored tranquility to the town. On Monday, what few remained of the rioters, took their course towards King's Norton, Bromsgrove, and Hales-Owen, where, split into small parties, they levied contributions on the peasantry. On Tuesday night, a body of them had assaulted Mr. Male's house, at Belle Vue, near the Leasowes; the Earl of Aylesford, with Justice Woodcock, and a few of the light dragoons, hastened thither. The people of the neighbourhood had, however, before their arrival, overpowered the rioters, and secured ten of them. Upon this his Lordship returned with the troops, and we believe that the lawless banditti, which had the two preceding days so much terrified the country, made their last appearance in any numbers here.

Many houses in the town and neighbourhood (besides those already enumerated) partially suffered, but were saved from destruction, either by persuasion, or by the gift of money or liquor; among these are the houses of Mr. T. Russell, near Moseley; of Mr. Harry Hunt, at Lady-wood; of the Rev. Mr. Coates, at the Five-ways; and Mr. Smith's house (Hay-hall). Mr. Jukes having intimation that his house in the Green Lanes was to be attacked, removed all his furniture, liquors, &c., took out his sashes and window frames, and conveyed whatever the rioters were likely to pull down, to a place of security. Owing to this judicious conduct, and the remonstrances and singular exertions of the Rev. Mr. Darwell, the house was saved from destruction.

On Wednesday three troops of the 11th regiment of light dragoons, and on Friday three troops of the 1st regiment of dragoon guards, marched into the town. Colonel de Lancey, with an Aid du Camp, arrived on Tuesday, from the King, to take the command of the military; and such was his Majesty's anxiety to provide for the security of this neighbourhood, that he had given orders for four

thousand

thousand troops to march to our relief from different quarters. About 500 of the 31st regiment of foot, and three troops of the Oxford Blues have since arrived, and still remain with us.

The Magistrates were assisted by the Earl of Aylesford, the Earl of Plymouth, Capt. Finch, Sir Robert Lawley, Mr. Cecil, Mr. Moland, Mr. Digby, Mr. Holbeche, Mr. Dixon, Mr. Lewis, Mr. Woodcock, &c., to whom the town is under great obligations.

Immediately on the restoration of tranquility, the following advertisement appeared in the Birmingham Gazette.

" The Dissenters of Birmingham desire to return their grateful acknowledgments, to all those members of the Established Church who in any manner exerted themselves during the late Riots, in defence of their persons or property; more particularly to those who, in the true spirit of Christianity, received into their houses, and under their protection, many families of Dissenters who were obliged to leave their own habitations; and also to all those who received and protected their goods. They trust that good men of every denomination, will consider this protection as highly honourable to the humanity of those who gave it, and they think it to be the more meritorious, as these generous protectors did thereby expose themselves to danger from a lawless mob, who wanted only *pretence* for depredation."

The same paper likewise contained the following:

" Notice is hereby given, That a Special Meeting of several of his Majesty's Justices of the Peace, for the counties of Warwick and Worcester, will be held at nine o'clock, this morning, at the Swan Inn, Birmingham, to receive *information respecting the late Riots;* and all persons that have it in their power to give any evidence relative thereto, are desired then and there to give their attendance.

" *Birmingham, July* 25, 1791."

Accordingly several magistrates for the above counties met, who were assisted by an eminent Counsel from London, the Solicitor to the Treasury, and Mr. Justice Bond; when, after receiving many depositions, they committed fifteen of the rioters to Warwick and Worcester county prisons; and issued out warrants for the apprehending of many others, who have absconded.

His Majesty was also graciously pleased to proclaim a reward of 100l. on the conviction of the instigators, and principals in these riots.

AN

AN AUTHENTIC ACCOUNT OF

The Trials of the Rioters at Warwick,

IN THE YEAR 1791;

INCLUDING THE JUDGE'S CHARGE,

AND THE

Speeches of the different Counsellors sent by Government.

[From Short-hand Minutes taken in Court.]

The Assizes at Warwick began on Monday, Aug. 22,—Mr. Baron *Perryn* came into Court about eleven o'clock, and the Grand Jury being sworn, he addressed them in the following terms:

"*Gentlemen of the Grand Jury,*

"YOU are now assembled here in order to perform a duty of a nature the most weighty and important—you are to enquire into all the crimes and offences, and your presentments are to be founded on the evidence that shall be given before you. Gentlemen, of the prisoners now in custody, there are many who are charged with being concerned in the late dreadful riots in Birmingham. In these riots *two dissenting meeting-houses*, and several other buildings were destroyed, to the alarm not only of this country, but of the kingdom in general. I need not tell you that riots are improper, but it is my duty to recommend these charges to your particular consideration. The law declares that insurrections for real or imaginary grievances, which shall have for their object the destruction of houses by force, shall be deemed high-treason.— Unhappily, not a few instances does our history furnish of the country being thrown into anarchy and confusion by insurrections, which, therefore, it is the duty of every one to assist in preventing, lest this Constitution (certainly the best in the world) should be ruined and destroyed.

"The Legislature to prevent riots, passed in the 1st of Geo. I. an act called the *Riot Act*. By this Act is declared, that if more than twelve persons shall assemble together, and shall refuse to disperse within one hour after they shall be required to do so by a Justice of the Peace, they shall be deemed guilty of felony without the benefit of Clergy. And by a clause in the same act, it is provided, that if persons assembled together shall begin to pull down any building, they shall likewise be said to be guilty of felony, although *no* Justice of Peace shall require them to separate. On *this* clause the charges against the prisoners now in custody are to be founded. After having thus stated this law to you, I cannot refrain from expressing my wonder and astonishment, that when all religious persecution had ceased, and toleration was extended to all, that such a period

should

should have been chosen for the commencement of persecution, and for the commission of every species of violence and desolation. Whatever circumstances might occasion these insurrections, nothing can justify them. British subjects of every persuasion, either in politics or religion, are equally entitled to the protection of the law. To you, Gentlemen, the care of the public tranquility is entrusted. —I will not detain you longer from the performance of your duty, further than to express my firm reliance on your wisdom, your justice, and your discretion."

Francis Field, alias *Rodney*, labourer, late of the parish of Aston, near Birmingham, was indicted for *Arson*, viz.: That he, not having the fear of God before his eyes, &c., did, on the 15th of July last, wilfully and maliciously set fire to the house of John Taylor, Esq., in the aforesaid parish, and at the same time did burn the said house, against the statute.

Mr. Newnham, counsel for the prosecution, stated, that it was his peculiar province, in the situation in which he stood, to support the present prosecution on the grounds which he should proceed to lay before the Jury. The prisoner was charged with setting fire to, and burning Mr. Taylor's house on that day, in which every person must know such tumultuous and dangerous riots took place as were a scandal and reproach to any well regulated government. It was not in the power of the magistrates, or other well disposed persons to withstand them. They were borne down by the tide of tumult, and Justice herself was overwhelmed by the rapid rush of violence and desolation. To such an excess were these riots carried that his Majesty, in order to preserve the property of his subjects in future, had taken them up as an act of government. Compassion certainly might be entertained for the prisoner, who, with others, in the frenzy of delusion, demolished one of the most elegant structures in the county of Warwick; yet that ought not to be suffered to operate so far as to acquit him of the crime imputed to him, if it should be proved in evidence that he had been guilty of it. Vicissitudes of opinions had often been known to produce the grossest insults on the government of this country. In the Riots in 1780, the capital was threatened with destruction, and was lighted up from one end to the other, by fires kindled solely by the frenzy of opinion. The habitation of Mr. Taylor still smoked in its ruins. The prisoner at the Bar was charged with setting fire to it—what might be his opinion, he would not pretend to state, nor was it of any importance, but this assertion he would make, that the only safe anchor of the constitution was the Law. Without that general protector of property and life, without that sheet-anchor of protection and hope, all would be subject to the assumed tyranny of opinions imposed by any tumultuous rabble whatever.—He concluded with observing, that if the charges brought against the prisoner should be proved by the evidence, it would be unnecessary for him to suggest to the Jury what ought to be done—because well was he convinced, that they would do what a Jury ought to do, their duty.

The following witnesses were called:

Edward Cotterell said he lived at Deritend, in the parish of Aston, near Birmingham. On the 15th of July he was at the house of Mr. Taylor, at three o'clock, where he stayed till five. Many persons were about the house, but no mischief was done between those two hours. At seven o'clock he returned to Mr. Taylor's, and found a larger number of people there than before. At eight o'clock they began to break the windows and to enter the house. The prisoner was among them: he went upstairs, where he remained some time. About half past nine he saw him again, throwing the frames of the windows, and some pieces of bedstead into the fire. He did not however know who lighted the fire, or when it was lighted.

Samuel Healy confirmed the testimony of the last witness.—In order to burn the house, fire-brands were carried from a public-house in the lane to Bordesley (the name of Mr. Taylor's seat) and set before the house; on this fire the furniture was thrown from the chamber windows, and soon after a fire was kindled in the Hall. The prisoner coming down stairs gathered some fire-brands in his hand, and carried them up stairs into one of the rooms; a second time he came down for a similar purpose, and conveying fire with him up stairs again, threw it into another room; he then set the staircase on fire at the landing place. During all this time he (witness) was in the house, but the fire beginning to rage with great fury, he was obliged to depart with as much speed as possible. In order to make the flame ascend with more rapidity, the prisoner ripped the paper from off the walls, threw it with some broken furniture into the fire, and stirred it with a staff he had in his hand; about eleven o'clock the roof fell in, in consequence of the different fires kindled in the several chambers and on the staircase. He swore to the person of the prisoner, whom he had seen several times in Birmingham, previous to this transaction. He also said that during the present transaction he was drunk.

In his cross examination he declared that he saw Field go up stairs, and that the fire in the Hall did not burn the house, because it was paved with flags. The roof fell in, in consequence of the fire carried up stairs by the prisoner.

John Brookes corroborated the evidence of the last witness.—He saw the prisoner throw the furniture into the fire before the house, but he did not see him throw any fire into the parlour.—He beheld him however, deposit some window-cases in the first floor, at which time the house was on fire.

Solomon Gardner proved that Mr. Taylor's house was in good

condition

condition before the 15th of July, and that at the expiration of that night it was burnt down.—No witnesses were called by the prisoner's Counsel.

His lordship, after entering particularly into the evidence given by each, declared that it was no mitigation of the prisoner's guilt that he was drunk—no man could exculpate himself from one crime by the committing of another.

As the Jury was on the point of retiring, one of the Jurymen stated to the Judge, that he entertained doubts relative to Healy's evidence. He had once been his servant, and he knew him to be possessed of very little veracity.

Baron PERRYN, replied that of the degree of credit to be attached to Healy's evidence the Jury must judge. Nothing had appeared on the trial to impeach his testimony.—He advised the jury, however, to retire, and then the gentleman who entertained doubts might suggest them more fully.—After being absent an hour, the Jury found the prisoner—*Guilty.*

[During the absence of the Jury, John Edwards and Walter Underwood were committed by his Lordship into the custody of the Gaoler, for threatening Joseph Elwell with "*a damn'd good licking,*" if he appeared an evidence against the rioters].

William Rice, late of the parish of Aston, near Birmingham, was indicted, for that he, with other persons, to the number of twenty and more on the 16th of July last, in the parish aforesaid, with force of arms, riotously and maliciously did assemble together to the disturbance of the public peace; and being assembled unlawfully and with force, did *begin* to pull down and demolish the house of Mr. *William Hutton,* contrary to the Statute, &c.

In a short introductory speech, Mr. Newnham stated, that this indictment differed from the last, inasmuch as the prisoner was charged with being engaged in those riots which, in the knowledge of every one, had produced such an alarm to the town of Birmingham in general, and such losses to many of its inhabitants.—Mr. Hutton was Commissioner and President of the Court of Requests in Birmingham: why he had been marked out as the devoted victim of the fury of these rioters, had not been disclosed nor even guessed at. In the destruction of his house, the prisoner had not only been present, and comforting the rioters, but he had also aided and assisted them.— Two witnesses stated themselves to have been hired by Mr. Hutton to stay and guard his house on the 15th of July last, as he apprehended that the mob would destroy it. Between four and five o'clock on the morning of the 16th, a mob came, huzzaing and crying "*Church and King for ever,*" and demanded liquor; that was given them, and they went away. At six they returned, with the prisoner and another at the head of them. On being requested to spare the

building

building, they replied, "*Damn them, it shall come down.*" Accordingly the windows were first broke to pieces, and the prisoner entering the house, proceeded to pull down the bannisters, and do other damage to the house, which was in a short time destroyed by fire.

On the part of the prisoner an *alibi* was set up.

George Rowell swore, that between four and five o'clock in the morning of the 16th of July, he was going to see the ruins of Mr. Taylor's house; on his way he met the prisoner, who went with him to one Tart's, where they parted about six.

George Mascall saw the prisoner at his house about half-past six o'clock, on the morning of the 16th of July. He came with several other persons, who, behaving in a riotous manner, were reprimanded by the prisoner, who swore that he would strike any one who attempted to injure the property of the witness. At his house they remained till about seven o'clock, when the prisoner went to the left, and the others to the right. The left was contrary to Mr. Hutton's house, which was then on fire.——The Jury found the prisoner—*Not Guilty.*

Robert Whitehead was tried for the same offence for which the last prisoner was indicted.

The same evidence was produced in this as in the last trial, with this addition, that the prisoner wrenched a gun from one of the witnesses, knocked him down, and would have murdered him, but for the intervention of another person. All the evidence on the part of the crown swore to the prisoner's person, and to his activity in demolishing Mr. Hutton's house.

On behalf of the prisoner,

James Moulds (though one of the persons who first informed Mr. Hutton of the prisoner's activity in destroying his house) was examined, who contradicted the evidence for the prosecution *in toto*. He said that the prisoner endeavoured to prevent the mob from doing any damage to Mr. Hutton's house; that he took the gun from the witness for the Crown, because he seemed to dare the mob with it; and struck him only with a stick. Moulds also declared that the prisoner did not break any of the windows, but tried to preserve Mr. Hutton's property.

Some witnesses gave the prisoner an excellent character.

Baron PERRYN, after particularizing the evidence, stated, that it rested with the Jury to decide, whether they thought the *four* witnesses produced by the Crown were to be believed in preference to the *one* witness (James Moulds) produced by the prisoner?—The Jury brought in their verdict—*Not Guilty.*

John Green, John Clifton, and *Bartholomew Fisher,* were indicted for that they, with one *Wm. Jones*, at large, and many others, did

riotously

riotously assemble on the 15th of July last, and begin to pull down the dwelling-house of Joseph Priestley, LL.D.

Mr. Coke, counsel for the prosecution, addressed the Jury in the following words:

"Gentlemen, You are now going to enter upon the same important business which engaged your attention yesterday.—The prisoners at the bar stand indicted for having assisted in demolishing the house of Dr. Priestley. That house, and all that perished during the riots, were sacrificed because they were the property of Dissenters. Gentlemen, I am far from adopting the opinions of Dr. Priestley; but notwithstanding this, I do not the less respect his moral character; I believe him to be exemplary in the discharge of every private and social virtue. Neither do I rank myself among Dissenters; on the contrary, I am a friend to our present religious establishment, but at the same time I do not hesitate to declare, that the Dissenters are a respectable and peaceable body of subjects. It is solely on account of their *opinions* that they have been thus infamously persecuted. I call it *persecution;* for if any thing deserves that title it is the cruel and unmerited attack they have lately sustained; Gentlemen, if this be a country in which men are to be persecuted for their opinions, I am sure it is a country not worth living in, and every man of spirit and understanding will sell his property, and seek for an asylum elsewhere. It is to you, Gentlemen, that the eyes of the whole kingdom are turned, for the punishment of the criminals who have been active in this persecution. I do not arraign you for any verdict you may have already given, but I intreat you to remember the nature of your office, and the solemn oath that you have taken. Dr. Priestley, whatever his sentiments may be, is entitled to the protection of the law; it is true, that I differ from his sentiments, both theological and political, but had I been in Birmingham on the night of the 14th of July, I would have lost my life in defence of his property; and I would have sacrificed it the more readily on account of our difference in opinion. Had the Dr. continued in his house but one half hour longer, what would have been the consequence? he must have perished in the flames which consumed his property—and then what an exchange would society have made! would the loss of Dr. Priestley be compensated by the lives of an hundred such miscreants as now stand at the bar?—In the course of next year there will be another 14th of July, and probably there will be another meeting; nor can it be denied but gentlemen have a right to meet and dine together if they please: but if you acquit the perpetrators of the late riots, consider the dreadful outrages to which your conduct may encourage them to proceed.—Remember, Gentlemen, that persecution invariably promotes the cause of the persecuted; it cements the suffering party in a stricter bond of union: I call upon you, therefore, as friends to the Church, to discourage it as far as you are able, by being impartial in your verdicts. Consider also, that in course of time some of your posterity may be subjected to persecution, and reflect what an example you will leave to future Juries if you are neglectful of your duty in the present instance, and if you verify that disgraceful report which is now circulating in Warwick, "that the Jury are determined to acquit all the rioters."

[Here he was interrupted by a Juryman, who objected to his mentioning the report; but the Judge, on being appealed to, said he saw nothing improper in it, and that he would not stop him.]

The Foreman of the Jury then rose to complain, that Mr. Coke had cast a reflection on their conduct, and that he had come there determined to do his duty. Very well, sir, replied the Judge, the Counsel is doing *his duty*, do you *do yours*.

Mr. Coke exculpated himself from the charge, by saying, he believed the report was without foundation; and then proceeded to call the evidence.

John Harris said he was present on the night of the 14th of July, when Dr. Priestley's friends were giving liquor to about thirty persons assembled before his house, who were, after some time, persuaded to go away. Soon, however, did they return, with increased numbers, broke the doors and windows to pieces, and entered the house. Green and Fisher were among the mob, and very active in destroying the building. Clifton was also there, but he saw very little of him, because he was employed in removing some of the furniture to a place of safety. About twelve the next day the mob set fire to the house, and burnt it. In his cross-examination, he said that he did not see the prisoners there the first time the mob came, or when they began to demolish the house.

Joseph Foster confirmed the evidence given by the last witness, as did *Alexander Clarke*.

In summing up the evidence Baron PERRYN declared that he did not think the evidence was strong enough to affect *Clifton*.———The Jury found *Green* and *Fisher—Guilty*, and *Clifton—Not Guilty*.

John Stokes, for beginning to pull down the Old Meeting-house in Birmingham, was *acquitted* on account of a defect in the indictment. In the register of the Meeting-house in 1689, it was stated to be situated in Philips-street; whereas, in the indictment, it was said to be in Old Meeting-house Lane.

William Shuker was indicted for beginning to pull down the dwelling-house of John Ryland, Esq., in Birmingham.

Joseph Elwell stated that he was present when the mob was destroying the house of Mr. Ryland. The prisoner who was the

Cryer

Cryer of Birmingham, was amongst the mob, ringing his bell, and crying, "*Damn the Presbyterians, down with them, burn them.*" He assisted in carrying away the wainscotting, and setting fire to the house.

John Hipkiss saw the prisoner in one of the rooms of Mr. Ryland's house, while the mob were demolishing the house. He did not see, however, any thing in his hand, but he said, "*Damn it, down with it.*"

John Luff swore also that the prisoner was active in destroying Mr. Ryland's house; that he received wainscotting and furniture from the people in the house, carried it away, and afterwards set fire to the house.

Mr. *Kenrick* swore to some expressions made use of by the prisoner, relative to his having set fire to the house.

On behalf of the prisoner, several witnesses contradicted part of the evidence of the first witness for the prosecution, and declared John Luff was a man not to be believed on his oath.

The Judge therefore stated to the Jury, that on account of this impeachment of the testimony of the two most material witnesses, no credit ought to be given to their evidence; with regard to Mr. *Kenrick's* evidence, he conceived it not to be of material importance in the present case, because it related to another supposed fact, viz., the prisoner's having set fire to Mr. Ryland's house.——*Acquitted.*

Joseph Careless was indicted for beginning to pull down the dwelling-house of John Ryland, Esq., on the 15th of July.

Mr. *Newnham* opened the case to the Jury. Hitherto, he said, in the conduct of these prosecutions, which his Majesty had directed to be at the expence of the public, he had, and should still refrain from stating anything, which might, in the judgment of any one, excite improper passions. He wished only to remind the Jury, that these prosecutions were not carried on for vindictive motives, but merely for the sake of public justice, and to read this lesson to all his Majesty's subjects, that his government, and the peace of all his subjects through his wide domains, was not to be interrupted by a lawless rabble and tumultuous riots. Not for the suffering Mr. Ryland, or for the prisoner, was he chosen to conduct these prosecutions, but to inform the world, that his Majesty and his Ministers meant nothing more but to make known, that in times of public riot, his ministry and his government would stand forth as the assertors and protectors of the English law. That law is the tenure by which all possess what is most dear to them. By that security, not by the capricious will of a tumultuous mob, do British subjects live. He had before stated that the exertions of the magistrates, and others, could not quell these riots. It remained for the slow-pacing step of the law, which though it had leaden heels, had iron hands. He should wave all comments on the alarm of the inhabitants of Birmingham, and proceed merely to state the fact, desiring the Jury only to decide according to the evidence, whether the prisoner was guilty or not. The prisoner had been charged with beginning to demolish the house of Mr. Ryland. He had been stated to be the ringleader of the mob, and to have encouraged them by saying, "*Come along, my lads, we will destroy that house.*"—If this fact were proved, it could not be doubted what ought to be done. The Gentlemen of the Jury would bear in mind that whenever a Jury departed from the evidence, from that time the law became not only uncertain, but useless. He demanded a verdict according to the evidence alone, and he expected that, listening to their oaths and the testimony produced before them, they would pursue that line of conduct which their duty prescribed.

Thomas Cooper stated, that he was at Mr. Ryland's house on the 15th of July last, and saw the prisoner among the mob, crying "*Church and King.*" He saw him throw bricks and stones up to the window, and fetch bottles of liquor out of the house, exclaiming at the same time, "*Come, my lads, we'll soon have it down.*" Several other persons were also very riotous.

Thos. Parker saw the prisoner at Mr. Ryland's, with a long rail, knocking down the bricks of a bow window belonging to the house.

Eliz. Grice (sister in law to the prisoner) contradicted the evidence of these two witnesses. She said that she saw the prisoner at Mr. Ryland's house; that he attempted to let some pigs out of a stye near the house, to prevent their being burnt; that he also threw from an out-house some trusses of hay and straw for the same purpose; for this conduct the mob threw fire at him.

Baron PERRYN remarked to the Jury, that two witnesses had given testimony against the prisoner, which was clear, distinct, and uncontradictory; a single witness, on the part of the prisoner, stood in opposition to their evidence. She had said that the prisoner attempted to save the pigs and the hay and straw. If that were true, he certainly had no idea of saving Mr. Ryland's property when he broke the brick-work of the bow-window with the iron rail. It remained, however, with the Jury to decide whether they would believe two or one.——*Not Guilty.*

Wm. Hands, alias *Hammonds*, indicted for a similar offence.

Mr. *Newnham* declared that he rose up with very serious impressions, and with a great deal of feeling which he would endeavour to stifle as much as he could. With the utmost deference, and under the correction of the Court, he begged leave to state to the Jury, that their only guide ought to be the solemn oaths they had taken, and the evidence. This was no common case. It was one in which the public safety was interested and involved. He entreated the Gentlemen to remember that in the late riotous proceedings the prisoner and his assistants had no feelings of compassion or humanity; they carried into excess the purpose of desolation and destruction, for which they were assembled; if, however, in opposition to the law, the Jury conceived that they were not called upon to decide according to evidence that had not been impeached; if they thought that judgment ought not to be founded on proof that might be adduced before them, he could only express a wish that they might sleep quiet in their beds.

James Trueman went on the 15th of July last to the house of Mr. Ryland, between three and four o'clock in the afternoon. A great number of people were assembled round it, among whom was the prisoner, whom he saw knocking the window cases to pieces with a piece of wood. The building was afterwards consumed by fire.

Job Harvey confirmed the testimony of the last Witness. He saw the prisoner also in the inside of the house pulling up the boards of the floor of one of the rooms and throwing them on the fire. The prisoner called no witnesses.——*Guilty.*

James Watkins was indicted for the same offence.

Nathaniel Addock was at Mr. Ryland's house on the 15th of July, from five till seven o'clock in the evening. He saw a great mob assembled, and the prisoner knocking the back door to pieces with an axe. Many were rioters; others looked on.——In his cross-examination he was not able to ascertain the number of persons engaged in demolishing Mr. Ryland's house—there were about *ten*, but he could not swear to more.

Mr. *Willis* therefore contended, on the part of the prisoner, that the indictment could not be supported, and that the prisoner ought to be acquitted. For the Act on which the indictment is founded says, "That if any persons to the number of twelve, or more, shall be assembled," &c. Evidence had only been produced of ten.

The Counsel for the prosecution replied, that, in a riot, proof of more than three was sufficient.

Baron *Perryn* declared, that he understood the number should be twelve; for though one of the clauses says *three*, the Act commences by fixing the number at twelve. In prosecutions for the Crown, it was always proper not to push any statute too far. However, he thought the case should be left to the Jury, who he was convinced from their conduct *would not convict the prisoner against the evidence*. But waving the strict law, he did not think the case so clear in point of evidence. If, however, the Jury found the prisoner guilty, he would reserve the construction of the Act of Parliament for the opinion of the Twelve Judges.——The Jury acquitted the prisoner.

Daniel Rose, aged 16, for beginning to destroy the house of *John Taylor*, Esq.

Mr. *Newnham* declined calling evidence against him, on account of his youth, and the hope that he might yet be useful to society.—— The prisoner was of course acquitted.

Those found *Guilty* were called to the Bar to receive sentence.

Baron *Perryn* then addressed them in the following Speech:

" *Francis Field,* you have been convicted of feloniously setting fire to the house of *John Taylor,* Esq.—*John Green* and *Bartholomew Fisher,* you have been found guilty of beginning to demolish the house of *Dr. Priestley*; and you, *William Hands,* have been convicted of beginning to destroy the house of *John Ryland,* Esq. Your offences, prisoners, alarmed the whole kingdom.—They are novel, and of such a nature, that you cannot expect the least mercy. The execution of the law is but a debt of humanity, as well as justice, due to the public, and to preserve in future the property of individuals from depredations, it is necessary that you should suffer. All the service I can now render you is, to entreat you to employ the short time permitted you to live, in a manner that may ensure you a happy eternity. Remember, unhappy and deluded men, that the certainty of death requires immediate repentance!

" The most painful part of my office now remains for me to perform. It is to pronounce the sentence, the *dreadful* sentence of the law, which is, That you go from hence to the place from whence you came, and from thence to the place of execution, where you shall be hanged by the neck till you are dead; and may the Almighty, of his infinite goodness, have mercy on your souls."

Field and Green were executed at Warwick, pursuant to the above sentence, on Thursday, Sept. 8.—Fisher received a free pardon, and Hands a respite for fourteen days.

The two following Addresses have been lately presented to the King:

To the KING's most excellent Majesty.

The humble Address of the High Bailiff, Clergy, and other principal Inhabitants of the Town and Neighbourhood of Birmingham.

" May it please your Majesty,

"WE, your Majesty's most dutiful and loyal subjects, the High Bailiff, Clergy, and other principal Inhabitants of the Town and Neighbourhood of Birmingham, deeply sensible of your Majesty's paternal care of all your subjects, beg leave most humbly to approach your Royal Throne, with hearts full of gratitude for the recent instance of that care which your Majesty graciously condescended to afford us during the late riots in this place, by commanding

manding such particular attention to be paid to our security, and directing such ample relief for our necessities.

"Rejoicing also in every opportunity of testifying our loyalty to the best of Sovereigns, and our firm attachment to that noble fabric the Constitution of this country, the envy of all other nations, as it is the glory of our own; We cannot neglect this occasion of pledging ourselves to support your Majesty's Illustrious House, and to defend that happy Constitution both in Church and State, against every attempt at innovation, at the risk of every thing dear to us."

To the KING.

"Most Gracious Sovereign,

"WE, your Majesty's loyal and dutiful subjects, the Protestant Dissenters in the Town of Birmingham, beg leave to approach your Majesty in a moment of serious affliction and concern, arising not only from our recent aggravated sufferings, but from our painful apprehensions lest the calumnies of our enemies should influence your Royal mind, and insinuate suspicions of our loyalty and affection.

"Assured not of our innocence alone, but of our unalterable attachment to your august person, and to the succession of your Royal House, we respectfully claim your Majesty's continued protection and favour, and beg leave most earnestly to assure your Majesty, we have no thoughts of disturbing the Constitution.—We are the descendants of those to whom (as the annals of our country will testify) the Revolution, which secured to your illustrious house the crown of these kingdoms, was greatly indebted. The civil constitution of our country is our pride and our glory; which we have been taught from our infancy to revere, and which we would die to preserve. Indeed, Sire, though deeply afflicted by the late riotous devastations, and by the want of energy in the civil power, yet we speak from hearts that are actuated by the love of law, of peace, of order, and good government. Sensible of your Majesty's goodness, in the vigorous measures which have been adopted for suppressing the outrages, which a lawless banditti were spreading through this place and its environs, we offer you the warmest tribute of our gratitude, for the happy deliverance we have experienced, by the wisdom of the measures planned by your Majesty's ministers, and by the energy and promptitude with which they were so successfully executed.

"We feel ourselves deeply thankful to your Majesty, for this very beneficial and decisive instance of your royal attention; and likewise to your great goodness, in the measures which have since

been

been adopted, for discovering and bringing to exemplary punishment, as well the instigators as the perpetrators of the late atrocious violences; and we firmly and dutifully rely upon your Majesty for the continuance of it, as well as for the exercise of that candour and magnanimity, which will resist the calumnies of our enemies, and continue to us that protection, favour, and confidence, to which we know ourselves justly entitled.

"That your Majesty may long reign in peace and glory; that your royal honours may for ages continue to descend to your latest posterity; and that the happiness of Britain may prosper and improve itself under their auspicious influence, is the honest wish and fervent prayers of, Sire,

"Your Majesty's most loyal and dutiful subjects."

LETTERS, &c. &c.

OCCASIONED BY THE LATE RIOTS.

Dr. Priestley to the Inhabitants of Birmingham.

My late Townsmen and Neighbours,

AFTER living with you eleven years, in which you had uniform experience of my peaceful behaviour, in my attention to the quiet studies of my profession, and those of philosophy, I was far from expecting the injuries which I and my friends have lately received from you. But you have been misled. By hearing the Dissenters, and particularly the Unitarian Dissenters, continually railed at, as enemies to the present Government, in Church and State, you have been led to consider any injury done to us as a meritorious thing; and not having been better informed, the means were not attended to. When the *object* was right, you thought the *means* could not be wrong. By the discourses of your teachers, and the exclamations of your superiors in general, drinking confusion and damnation to us (which is well known to have been their frequent practice) your bigotry has been excited to the highest pitch, and nothing having been said to you to moderate your passions, but every thing to inflame them; hence, without any consideration on your part, or on theirs, who ought to have known, and taught you better— you were prepared for every species of outrage; thinking that whatever you could do to spite and injure us, was for the support of Government, and especially the Church. In *destroying* us, you have been led to think, *you did God* and your country the most substantial *service*.

Happily, the minds of Englishmen have an horror of *murder*, and therefore you did not, I hope, think of *that*; though, by your

clamorous

clamorous demanding of *me* at the Hotel, it is probable, that at that time, some of you intended me some personal injury. But what is the value of life, when every thing is done to make it wretched. In many cases, there would be greater mercy in despatching the inhabitants, than in burning their houses. However, I infinitely prefer what I feel from *the spoiling of my goods*, to the disposition of those who have misled you.

You have destroyed the most truly valuable and useful apparatus of philosophical instruments that perhaps any individual, in this or any other country, was ever possessed of; in my use of which I annually spent large sums, with no pecuniary view whatever, but only in the advancement of science, for the benefit of my country, and of mankind. You have destroyed a library corresponding to that apparatus, which no money can re-purchase, except in a long course of time. But what I feel far more, you have destroyed *manuscripts*, which have been the result of the laborious study of many years, and which I shall never be able to re-compose; and this has been done to one who never did, or imagined you any harm.

I know nothing more of the *hand-bill*, which is said to have enraged you so much, than any of yourselves, and I disapprove of it as much; though it has been made the ostensible handle of doing infinitely more mischief than any thing of that nature could possibly have done. In the celebration of the French Revolution, at which I did not attend, the company assembled on the occasion, only expressed their joy in the emancipation of a neighbouring nation from tyranny, without intimating a desire of any thing more than such an improvement of our own Constitution, as all sober citizens, of every persuasion, have long wished for. And though, in answer to the gross and unprovoked calumnies of Mr. Maden and others, I publicly vindicated my principles as a Dissenter, it was only with plain and sober argument, and with perfect good humour. We are better instructed in the mild and forbearing spirit of Christianity, than ever to think of having recourse to *violence;* and can you think such conduct as yours any recommendation of your religious principles in preference to ours?

You are still more mistaken, if you imagine that this conduct of yours has any tendency to serve your cause, or to prejudice ours. It is nothing but *reason* and *argument* that can ever support any system of religion. Answer our arguments, and your business is done; but your having recourse to *violence*, is only a proof that you have nothing better to produce. Should you destroy myself as well as my house, library, and apparatus, ten more persons, of equal or superior spirit and ability, would instantly rise up. If those ten were destroyed, an hundred would appear; and believe me, that the Church of England, which you now think you are supporting, has received a greater blow by this conduct of yours, than I and all my friends have ever aimed at.

Besides, to abuse those who have no power of making resistance, is equally cowardly and brutal, peculiarly unworthy of Englishmen, to say nothing of Christianity, which teaches us to do as we would be done by. In this business we are the sheep, and you the wolves. We will preserve our character, and hope you will change yours.

At all events, we return you blessings for curses; and pray that you may soon return to that industry, and those sober manners, for which the inhabitants of Birmingham were formerly distinguished.

I am your sincere well-wisher,

London, July, 19, 1791.   J. PRIESTLEY.

J. Keir, Esq., to the Printer of the Birmingham and Stafford Chronicle.

Mr. Printer,

AS I find that many gross falsehoods have been circulated through the country, in order to inflame the minds of the people concerning the meeting held last Thursday, to commemorate the French Revolution, I will beg leave to state what I myself have had occasion to know respecting that subject.—Some gentlemen in Birmingham had proposed by an advertisement in the newspapers, to hold a meeting of the friends of liberty and of mankind, at the Hotel, to commemorate the French Revolution, in the same manner as was done in London, and many other parts in the kingdom. Two days before the time appointed for this meeting, a very respectable gentleman called on me, and said he came to tell me, that it was the general wish of those who intended to meet, that I should be their chairman on the occasion. I accepted the compliment, and promised to come to Birmingham to attend, never conceiving that a peaceable meeting, for the purpose of rejoicing that twenty-six millions of our fellow-creatures were rescued from despotism, and made as free and happy as we Britons are, could be misinterpreted as being offensive to a government, whose greatest boast is liberty, or to any who profess the christian religion, which orders us to love our neighbours as ourselves.—We accordingly met and dined with the greatest peace and harmony, and after drinking some toasts, expressive in the first place of our loyalty to our own *King* and *Constitution*; and in the second place, of our joy at the happiness which the French have acquired by their new Constitution, we dissolved the meeting entirely, in the greatest order, between five and six in the evening, and quitted the Hotel, every man retiring separately to his home, or to his private affairs. I returned to my
house

house in the country, nor knew of the disturbances till next day. The meeting in London was conducted with the same decorum, nor has there been an instance, as far as I know, in the many similar meetings throughout England, of the smallest irregularity attempted by them. Now, Mr. Printer, as actions are the best interpreters of men's intentions, it is evident that the malicious insinuations, that these meetings were intended to disturb the peace and government of the country, have been by the event proved to be false and groundless.

I have lately heard that it is reported that we drank disloyal and seditious toasts. Now the very first toast that was given was, *The King and the Constitution.* I do not know any words in the English language expressive of greater loyalty; and one of the last was, *Peace and good-will to all mankind,* which cannot easily be interpreted to excite people to tumult. I shall hereafter publish a list of· all the toasts, which were altogether in the same spirit of loyalty, peace, and charity.

A second report is, that Justice Carles was insulted and turned out of the room. The fact is, that Justice Carles never was in the room, and therefore it is not easy to conceive how he could be turned out. I will add, that I have not the smallest doubt, that if that gentleman had come, he would have been received with due respect.

A third false report was, that a seditious hand-bill had been distributed by the members of the meeting, on some preceding day. A seditious and truly infamous hand-bill had been distributed, it is true, but by whom written or distributed is not known. It is heartily to be wished that the persons concerned may be discovered, and punished according to law. As soon as the gentleman of Birmingham who had concerted the Commemoration Meeting, saw this hand-bill, they perceived that the effect, and perhaps the intention of it, was to inflame the mob against them, and they immediately published in the Thursday's newspaper, an advertisement declaring their disavowal of this hand-bill, and their own loyal attachment to the *King, Lords,* and *Commons*.* They also sent hand-bills with copies of this advertisement all over Birmingham. It was not possible for them to do any thing more effectual to prevent any bad effects from this seditious paper, or to rescue themselves from the calumny of their being the authors of it.

The last false report that I have heard relative to that meeting, is concerning Dr. Priestley's behaviour there. To this I suppose it will be sufficient to answer, that *Dr. Priestley was not present.*

These are all the reports which I have heard, but I doubt not there may be many others, of the truth of which every man of common sense will judge from what I have said of those which have come to my knowledge. Nevertheless, these false reports are

·'all

* See Page 4.

all the pretences for the late horrible riots; but the event shews that they were only *pretences*, and that the Dissenters were the true object of the fury of the mob, as many of those gentlemen who have suffered from the riots were not present. For the business of the Commemoration meetings had nothing to do with religious distinctions, and were in other parts composed of churchmen, catholics, and dissenters. It is true that in Birmingham the majority were dissenters; but it is evident that they did not wish it to be distinguished as a party meeting, when they did me the honour to chuse* me as their chairman, who, it was evident, must have conformed, in order to qualify myself for the commissions which I have held in the army, to all the formalities prescribed by the Test Act, and who never was present in a dissenting meeting above once or twice in England; although I have the greatest regard for the dissenting individuals whom I know, among whom are several of the late unfortunate victims, men as peaceable, respectable, and loyal as any in the kingdom. But as the subject of the commemoration meeting was quite unknown to the ignorant part of the people, it gave an opportunity of raising any lies that were necessary to inflame the mob to execute their horrid purposes.—But that the proceedings of the meeting were innocent, peaceable, and honourable, and also free from every subject relative to religious parties, I solemnly affirm.

I am, Mr. Printer,
Yours, &c.   JAMES KEIR.

West Bromwich, July 20, 1791.

* Sic in original.

J. Keir, Esq. to the Printer of the Birmingham Gazette.

Mr. Printer,

I BEG leave to acquaint the public with the proceedings of the meeting, held at the Hotel, on the Fourteenth of July, for celebrating the French Revolution. As the toasts then drank have been wonderfully misrepresented, and brought into more consequence by the late riots than they otherwise would merit, I think it necessary to add such remarks as may be requisite to shew their true spirit and intent.

Eighty-one gentlemen, inhabitants of the town and neighbourhood, met at the great room in the Hotel, where they dined and passed the afternoon, with that social, temperate, and benevolent festivity, which the consideration of the great event, that has diffused happiness and liberty among a large portion of the human race, inspired.

It is but justice to the liberality and public spirit of an ingenious artist of this town, to mention, that he decorated the room upon this occasion, with three elegant emblematic pieces of sculpture, mixed with painting, in a new style of composition. The central piece was a finely executed medallion of his *Majesty, encircled with a glory,* on each side of which was an alabaster obelisk; one exhibiting *Gallic liberty* breaking the bonds of despotism, and the other representing *British liberty* in its present enjoyment.

The following toasts were drank, and were agreeably intermixed with songs, composed and sung by some of the company.

1. The King and constitution.

It is the duty of all loyal subjects to support the Constitution, as it is, even if there be some less perfect parts in which a reformation may be wished. But such a reformation ought to be wished to take place by legal means, and not by tumults. It was with the same view of reprobating all thoughts of introducing reformations by violence, that I had occasion, in a former publication* to remark upon Mr. Burke's pamphlet, that if he vilified the French Revolution in order to deter us from following the same example, his fears were unnecessary; because, " Happily the same necessity does not exist in this country. For although our government may not be the best *possible*, it is certainly too good to risk any public convulsion, in hopes of a better, or to attempt any other change than such as may naturally follow from the progressive advancement and extension of knowledge among the people, by which our constitution may rather be restored to its true principles, which are excellent, and farther improved and adapted to the cultivated genius of the age, than altered or overturned." These, then, were the sentiments which I declared and avowed in a time of more deliberation, and before the present occasion could suggest them; namely, that the principles of our constitution are excellent; and that the only reformation wanted, is such as shall restore the constitution to these principles, but shall not alter or overturn it; and that no reformation ought to be attempted with violence. If any one ask, what are these principles of the constitution that are excellent? I answer, it is the division of the sovereign power into three independent estates, King, Lords, and Representatives of the people. These principles require that the representation of the people should be equal, that is, that equal numbers should send an equal number of members to parliament; and upon these principles the constitution was originally formed; but the changes which time has introduced has unhinged all this equality. Old Sarum, now reduced to a single house, sends two members, while Birmingham, as a town with its 70,000 inhabitants, sends no representative. Little boroughs will generally sell their votes to the best bidder; large bodies of men cannot be bribed. A more equal representation is the only means of obtaining a more independent parliament, and has always been the object which the most independent and patriotic men in every part of England have endeavoured to obtain by petitions and remonstrances to parliament, but hitherto without success.

* Life of Mr. Day.

2. * The prosperity and immortality of the glorious system of Government ratified in the Champ de Mars on the ever memorable 14th of July, 1790.

3. The National Assembly and Patriots of France, whose virtue and wisdom have raised twenty-six millions from the mean condition of subjects of despotism, to the dignity and happiness of freemen.

4. The majesty of the people.

By this expression is meant the dignity and importance of the people, for whose good all governments ought to be instituted. The majesty of the people is a parliamentary expression.

5. May the New Constitution of France be rendered perfect and perpetual.

It is to be hoped that the French may improve their present constitution, the principal imperfection of which is the circumstance in which it differs from ours, namely, the want of a third estate, or House of Lords, to hold a balance between the King and the People. I wish to shew that the opinions delivered here are not suggested on this occasion, and I, therefore, must beg leave to add another quotation from my late publication (The Life of Mr. Day.) "Although the essential preliminaries to the firm establishment of a free constitution in France have been accomplished, much yet remains to be done towards its completion; and for this purpose, time and security are requisite.—Whatever judgment then we can form at present may be premature. Perhaps the apparently too democratic spirit of the present system may be hereafter qualified by the institution of a Senate or permanent Magistracy, similar in its effects to our House of Peers, to whom such privileges may be granted as shall be necessary for their independence, not as nobles, but as a body forming an essential part of the state; who, by poising the powers of the crown, and of the people, and by forming a barrier between the executive and legislative authorities, may keep these distinct, and give to the whole government the stability and dignity becoming a great empire."

As the French give a free scope to their reason in political discussions, not yet being divided into parties which have interests different from the general interest, we may hope at least for a greater perfection of the French constitution than has hitherto be seen, not only for a further extension and security of the happiness of that great people, but also that the governments of other nations, feeling the good effects of their institutions, may adopt whatever is wanting to render their own more perfect. With this view the following words had been added to the toast, "as a glorious example to all ages and nations;" but I did not pronounce them from the chair, from a notion which then struck me, that among so great a number some people might be so inaccurate as not to distinguish that the

---

* This Toast was not inserted in the original list, but was written on a separate piece of paper by the gentleman who proposed it. When Mr. Russell found it necessary to publish the Toasts in a London paper, he was obliged to omit this Toast, because he had not a copy of it, not having been inserted in the original list.

example

example is not proposed in the present imperfect state of the French constitution, but in the *perfect* state which does not exist, but is the object of the wish of the toast. From the circumstances that I have pointed out, in which the French constitution is inferior to our own, as well as from many other considerations, although I admire the French Revolution as a French Revolution, I heartily deprecate its imitation in Great Britain and Ireland.

6. May Great Britain, Ireland, and France, unite in perpetual friendship, and may their only rivalship be in the extension of peace and liberty, wisdom and virtue.

7. The rights of Man. May all nations have the wisdom to understand, and the courage to assert and defend them.

The rights of man extend to a freedom in every thing which does not interfere with the rights of his neighbour, or the good of the community, as expressed by law. It is clear, then, that they do not extend to the pulling down and burning of other men's houses.

8. The true friends of the constitution of this country; who wish to preserve its spirit by correcting its abuses.

The principal abuse is the unequal distribution of the power of electing members of Parliament, as was before observed.

9. May the people of England never cease to remonstrate, till their Parliament becomes a true National Representation.

Nothing can more fully shew the orderly and loyal sense of the meeting than this toast, which expresses, that however unremitting we should be in our endeavours to procure a reform in the representation of the people, it is only by *remonstrating*, that these endeavours are to be executed.

10. The Prince of Wales. May he have the wisdom to prefer the glory of being the chief of an entire and free people, to that of being the splendid fountain of corruption.

Although this toast has no reference to the past or present times, and expresses only a wish that in some future time, when it shall please God, in the ordinary course of nature, to call the Prince to his inheritance, he may have the wisdom to prefer good to evil; and that then, or before that time, the Parliament may have granted what the friends of Liberty have so often petitioned, a more perfect representation of the people, by means of which they will be the true and uncorrupt representatives of the entire nation, and the King will preside there as chief, with a splendour and dignity which a partial representation cannot give: it may, nevertheless, be not improper here to say something of that corruption, which has been often imputed to ministers, since the Revolution under King William; that is, the practice of bestowing places, pensions, honours, and other emoluments in the gift of the crown, for the purpose of obtaining influence and majorities in Parliament.—Before the Revolution, Kings governed by prerogative. When that was circumscribed, ministers found that they could not carry on the measures of Government without the consent

of

of Parliament, and that majorities were not always to be gained, without acquiring an influence by the choice which the Constitution gave them in the disposal of the favours of the crown. The fault then was evidently not in the ministers, but in the representatives, the majority of whom being chosen by little boroughs, instead of the great body of the people, rendered this influence necessary. Some political writers maintain, that influence is an admirable system of government: and it must be confessed that no nation ever enjoyed more liberty and happiness than this has done for the past century. But everything in this world has its limits. We have the authority of the celebrated vote of a House of Commons for saying, "that the influence of the crown has encreased, is encreasing, and ought to be diminished." According to this progression, may we not fear that unless some stop be put to it, in some future time, the crown may become what the toast deprecates, a splendid fountain of corruption. In the year 1780, associations were formed of the most patriotic and independent gentlemen in different counties of Engrand, to obtain a reform in Parliament, as the only remedy against this increasing evil. To give an idea of the corruption which then prevailed, it may not be improper to quote a passage of a memorial drawn up by the deputies of the county of York, Surrey, Middlesex, Gloucester, Hertford, Kent, Huntingdon, Dorset, Bucks, Chester, Devon, and Essex. "We are now arrived (said these deputies) at the crisis which the wisest of political writers have uniformly marked for the downfall of Britain," when the legislative body shall become as corrupt as the executive, and dependent upon it.—"Let any man look back to the laws which have passed only in the ten last sessions of Parliament, forming, as it were, step by step, a mode of prerogative, and then doubt if the executive has not found its way to the corruption of the legislative. Let him behold a venal majority in the House of Commons, session after session, moving obsequious to the nod of the minister, and giving the legislative sanction to propositions not only big with the fate of the country, but often militating against the first principles of the constitution, and the declared voice of their constituents; and then let him judge how enormous that corruption must be." It is well known that Mr. Pitt, his Majesty's present minister, wrote to the chairman of these deputies, the Rev. Mr. Wyvill, promising to move the House of Commons for a reform in the Parliamentary Representation, which promise he fulfilled, but though he was then minister, could not gain a majority. The time may nevertheless arrive, and what better omen can there be than the concurrence of the two heads of our political parts, Mr. Pitt and Mr. Fox, in this great question. Soon may it arrive to gild the setting sun of the present reign, and be the glory of every succeeding one!*

* In the list of Toasts published in the London papers by Mr. Russell, this toast is given, "The Prince of Wales," without the additional sentence. This difference arises from a mistake of mine. The toast in the original list was as Mr. Russell has given it. The additional sentence was proposed,

11. The United States of America. May they for ever enjoy the Liberty which they have so honourably acquired.

12. May the late Revolution in Poland prove the harbinger of a more perfect system of Liberty, extending to that great kingdom.

13. May the nations of Europe become so enlightened, as never to be deluded into savage wars, by the mad ambition of their rulers.

14. May the sword never be unsheathed but for the defence and liberty of our country, and then may every man cast away the scabbard, until the people are safe and free.

The man who will not fight in defence of his country, does not deserve the protection of it; and he who will not fight for liberty, deserves to be a slave—excepting those always, whose conscience forbids them to fight.

15. To the glorious memory of Hampden and Sydney, and other heroes, of all ages and nations, who have fought and bled for Liberty.

16. To the memory of Dr. Price, and of all those illustrious sage who have enlightened mankind on the true principles of civil society.

17. Peace and good-will to all mankind.

An admirable text, and I wish the christian preachers of all denominations would enforce it with all their eloquence. Let us remember that Churchmen and Dissenters are all made in the same mould, and subject to the same passions, and that the differences arise from education and accident; let us remember that the animosities among the good people of all parties, arise from the misconception of each other; let us all conspire in acquiring the sentiments expressed in the toast, and when once acquired, we shall certainly never abandon them.

18. Prosperity to the Town of Birmingham.

19. A happy meeting to all the friends of liberty, on the 14th of July, 1792.

I am, Mr. Printer, yours, &c.

July 24, 1791. JAMES KEIR.

To Messrs. Priestley and Russell.

YOU have both ventured a letter each in the public papers on the late dreadful riots, which have been committed in the Town of Birmingham, in order, I suppose, to excite commiseration for your situations, and to divert the public eye from yourselves to others, as the supposed cause of all those riots.———The minds of men are by this time cooled a little—and in answer to your artful and wicked

and written in the Chairman's list, but upon reconsideration it was ordered to be omitted, but forgot to be expunged; and in the hurry of the day, I pronounced it, by an unintentional mistake, for which I beg the indulgence of the gentlemen who directed the toasts. The additional sentence had never been inserted in Mr. Russell's list, and he therefore could not give it in London.

insinuations, I hope to prove to every dispassionate person in the kingdom, that you yourselves may be considered as the *real* cause of that mob, and those riots you so much complain of.

Your letter, *good* Doctor, opens with an appeal to the *uniform experience the town has had of your peaceful behaviour, and attention to the quiet studies of your profession, for the eleven years you have resided near it.*—Now it is notorious—that the town of Birmingham had enjoyed an uninterrupted scene of peace and happiness for more than fifty years: Every thing in it moved in perfect harmony and order, till you, like a noxious planet, approached towards it. Religious differences and divisions were few (from your own writings I can prove this) till *you* came to sow the seeds of dissension by your pestilential publications, and unfounded doctrines from the pulpit.— You have endeavoured to unhinge the minds of the people—to alienate their affections from government—from religious observances on the established church—from every attention and respect due to their appointed teachers and pastors—and to perplex their minds with subtle disputes on religious doctrines, in which your own creed, by your own confession, is not yet fixed.——These practices, you are conscious, have been your daily business—and yet you have the impudence to appeal to the uniform experience of the town of Birmingham for your *peaceful* behaviour, and attention to your *quiet* studies.—In proof of what has been said—I appeal to your own writings, to your unwearied attacks upon governors and our present established government—to your illiberal abuse of the whole body of the clergy—and I appeal not only to the town of Birmingham in general—but even to the more moderate dissenters there, who, I understand, at present impute all their sufferings to the violence and impetuosity of your nature, and the well-known restless spirit of your *busy Friend.*

To say, that the mob was misled, and their bigotry excited to the highest pitch, by hearing the dissenters railed at, and that the discourses of the clergy have led the people to think, that in *destroying you,* they did *God service,* is a bold and false assertion, without the least proof or truth.—And as you, Doctor, are, I understand, of so weak and irritable a nature, that the least contradiction agitates your whole frame, let me recommend it to you for your own peace of mind, to consult a little the truth of facts, before you make another attempt like this to impose upon the world—impose you cannot on the inhabitants of Birmingham, who know the *reverse* of what *you* assert to be the direct fact.—Considering the most violent and outrageous attacks you have made of late upon all establishments, and your eternal workings to undermine the church—a clergyman resident in the town of Birmingham would be wanting surely in the duties of his office, and in his regard to that church he is bound to serve, who suffered your unprovoked insolence and calumnies to pass unnoticed and

unmarked

unmarked—but the truth is, I believe, Doctor, that the clergy of Birmingham are a mild and peaceable set of men, who regard more the common duties of their office than your virulent abuse, which cannot move their anger, however it might excite their pity or contempt.—The people, you say, have been misled—but pray who has endeavoured to mislead them? Who? but Dr. Priestley—by his constant railing at the present government, both in church and state. *Who* has constantly taught that the *destruction of us* is a right object, and that the *means* could not be wrong, even the means of a *gunpowder* plot? The world knows it is Dr. Priestley.—*Who*, by his writings and discourses has endeavoured to excite and inflame the passions of the people, and prepare them for every species of outrage —but Dr. Priestley?—*Who* has led the people to think that in destroying the established church, they did God and their country the most substantial service? Who? but Dr. Priestley—in his Familiar Letters, his Answer and Preface to Mr. Burns, &c., &c.—*You had digged a pit, and are fallen into the midst of it yourself. In the net which you hid privily, is your foot taken—you are trapped in the work of your own hands—and the mischief you had imagined against another, is fallen upon your own head.* You must have understood very well, and felt the power of these wicked arts, to have been enabled with so much readiness to have attributed them to others.

Whether your conscience tells you that you deserve death, I know not—but by your words 'tis clear, that the misfortune of losing you, though of such service, *in your own opinion*, to society in general, would have been nothing in comparison of the many outrages committed on private property and effects.—And we entirely agree with you, Doctor.

The sufferings of a *good man* every one partakes of and laments— and those of Mr. *Taylor* and Mr. *Ryland*, in particular, and of others whose effects fell a sacrifice to the violences of the mob, are very generally lamented—but the sufferings of those who instigate evil that over-reaches themselves, carry too much the appearance of *deserved punishment* to excite commiseration.—You, Sir, in most modest language, have described your sufferings to be very great, in the destruction of the first and most useful apparatus of philosophical instruments that any man in this or any other country was ever possessed of.—Our feelings for you on this head would have been greater, had this description come from some other hand than your own.—In the loss of your *manuscripts*, there are some who think, that the misfortune of losing *one* part, is somewhat compensated in the destruction of *another*.

You deny any concern in the *hand bill*. No one, that I hear, has proved it upon you. Some, however, *did think*, it bore a striking *similarity* to your *usual* language.

The world only smiles at your palliation of yourself, in saying that you

you did not attend the celebration of the French Revolution. Being well acquainted with your principles, we are not at a loss for your meaning. No one is surprized at your revengeful introduction of Mr. *Madan*'s name. As he told you that you smarted under the lash of a superior hand, so we think you at present smart under the lash of *his telling you so.*—You are always very kind in your advice to *us*, how *we* are to direct our conduct, and what modes we are to take to serve our cause. We thank even an *enemy* for his advice—*when it is well meant.*

To whom now, Sir, in this letter of yours, have you been addressing yourself? To the inhabitants, I think, of the town of Birmingham.—And are you not ashamed to endeavour thus to asperse their characters in the world, when it is so true, that every nerve was exerted, both by the laity and clergy of the established church (to their honour be it mentioned) even at the hazard of their own lives and properties, to save and protect the property of the dissenters in the late riots. Have you no gratitude in you? If *you* have not, the *body of the dissenters have*—and their public thanks to the laity and clergy of the established church, in the Birmingham paper of the 25th of July, gave the directest contradiction to the whole catalogue of your most wicked insinuations and unfounded assertions.

You are a strong Revolutionist we all know.—For God's sake, for ours, and *your own*, since you reverence so much the Revolution system, get off for France. The people of Birmingham never wish more to see or hear of you, and England, I am sure, will be very glad to get rid of so troublesome a character. Your letter needed not the signature of *Priestley*.—Every one acquainted with the shameful, unqualified, and undignified manner in which you write in general, must know the hand from whence this came. The same mode of shuffling, misinterpreting, shifting, twisting, and uniform system of false statements, pervade every publication that comes from you.—Every man may now judge what reliance is to be placed on your *scripture* interpretations, from the specimen you have given us of your powers of perversion in the letter now before us.—*Quocunque modo* is your motto, when you have a point to carry.

———

To you, Mr. RUSSELL, my address will be very short. You are not of consequence sufficient to attract the public notice; and you are but the *bell-mouth* of Dr. Priestley. He probably composed what you and Mr. *Keir* have set your names to. You have been pleased, however, to vouch for *that* in the most solemn manner, which I affirm to be a direct *falsehood*. Before you ventured to publish *Toasts** given at your meeting, it was your business to be

* Mr. Russell's letter respecting the Toasts (published in London) is purposely omitted, as Mr. Keir has written so fully on that subject, and clearly accounts for Mr. Russell's inaccuracy in the statement of some of them, which is noticed with so much asperity by this Lover of Truth.—

acquainted

acquainted (and indeed *you must have been acquainted*, Mr. Russell) with those toasts in their full extent. Otherwise you aver that, which you cannot know to be true. Now Mr. *Keir*'s own publication of the toasts since your letter appeared, proves you to have been guilty of a gross falsehood.—The fact is, you were ashamed (as you ought to be) of *some* of your toasts, and you published, therefore, only a *part*, and that a *mutilated* one, hoping to escape detection. Unluckily for you and your party, we have as correct a copy as your worthy chairman, Mr. *Keir*—and I am told that even *he* has kept back some, and varied others; but this I affirm not on my own knowledge.—His letter is the most *jesuitical* comment on a *presbyterian* performance I ever saw.

You are brought to shame (though I give you too much credit, by supposing you possessed of any) for *one* falsehood.

Your representation of your conference with Mr. Dadley, the Master of the Hotel, carries with it *another* falsehood.

You would represent yourself and friends on this occasion, as taking every precaution, and lay the blame, in part, on poor Mr. Dadley, who is a very *innocent* and good kind of man, for assuring you, there would be no danger of any tumult, *if you took care only to break up early.*

Come forward, now, Sir, and deny the charge against you, if you can. You were the very man, who declared, in the most peremptory language, on a representation of the danger likely to ensue, that there *should* be a dinner; that if you sat down alone you would insist on it, and would be responsible for all consequences.———I leave you now, Sir, to make the best of these *charges* of *falsehood* against you—and to convince the world, if you can, that you and your party may not be considered as the *real* authors, by your obstinate perseverance in your meeting, against the sober cautions and general alarm of the whole town of Birmingham, of all those *dreadful riots* that ensued. I am, Messieurs, NOT the Button Burnisher, but,

A Lover of Truth.

A short Reply to Dr. Priestley.

SIR,

YOU have appealed to the Public in vindication of your conduct, and lamented your losses with the feelings of a man; they are great, because in one respect irreparable.

But whilst I join with the public in regretting the destruction of your philosophical property, it pains me to aver that you have not proved your political innocence.

Whether the declaration of Mr. Russell, respecting Mr. Dadley, is to be credited in preference to the *assertion* of an anonymous writer, is submitted to the Reader's consideration.——*Compiler.*

You and your friends have been charged as enemies to the present system of Government: let us examine how you attempt to disprove that assertion.

You say, that your friends met to express their joy at the French Revolution, and to intimate a desire that an improvement should take place in our Constitution.

Does the inference to be drawn from this, prove you, and those of your persuasion, to be friends to the present established Government?—Surely not.

By celebrating the French Revolution, you give your sanction to the system adopted in that country. If you did not sanction, you would celebrate: and by desiring an improvement, at the same moment, in the British Constitution, you declare yourself inimical to our Government in its present form. He who is inimical to any matter, cannot be a friend; and the opposite to that character is, of course, an enemy. Your letter has afforded me these premises, and the conclusion is fairly drawn from that which is fully established.

It is not your religious, but your political sentiments which are thought dangerous to the State. The Presbyterians certainly approve the conduct of that usurped authority which decolated the unhappy CHARLES. Our Constitution considers that bloody act of common-wealth tyranny, to be a martyrdom. The difference in political sentiment on this great point, can therefore never be reconciled. It is as opposite as Monarchy and Republicanism can make it. Were I to ask you, if the doctrine laid down by Mr. Paine in his *Rights of Man*, coincided with your principles?—you would certainly say that "it does." You cannot successfully controvert that assertion.

Now, Sir, this publication of Mr. Paine's is a gross libel upon the spirit and letter of the British Constitution, and as it is received into your community as a political truth, and that in approving such doctrine, you and your friends cannot disapprove the French Revolution, I wish to know what sort of amendment you would make to the British Government?

You have made a distinction in your letter, between the constitutional subjects of Great Britain and your sect. You divide them by saying, "our cause," and "your cause." The constitutional subjects' *cause*, is the present Government in Church and State,—your cause must be the opposite to that;—and therefore it is some other kind of Government in Church and State; and though you have not directly said that you ever attacked the State, you fairly acknowledge to have given our Church A BLOW:—Your words are, "The Church of England, which you now think you are supporting, has received a greater blow by this conduct, than I and all my friends *have ever aimed at it*." This is a direct avowal that you and your friends have aimed a blow at our religious rights.

Do

Do you call this *peaceably* following your studies as a Minister of the Gospel and a Philosopher?—No, Mr. Priestley, it is such kind of turbulent conduct that has brought you and your friends into the present situation.

Had you, Sir, and those of your persuasion, quietly attended the duties of your respective stations, and left the Protestant Church and the British Government to the care of those who are appointed by the Constitution, as Representatives of the People, to guard and protect them; you might have enjoyed that ease, happiness, and peace which every good subject is entitled to expect from the excellence of our laws, and the honour and integrity of those men who compose the three branches of the Legislature.

JOHN CHURCHMAN*.

July 20, 1791.

To the Inhabitants of the Town of Birmingham.

Friends and Fellow Townsmen,

IT is with extreme concern and reluctance that I offer a few remarks on the letter which has lately been addressed to us, in several London papers, under the signature of Dr. Priestley.

He complains of the injuries sustained by himself, and other very respectable individuals, in the late riots. The calamity has indeed been great; and while every benevolent mind must feel deeply for the sufferers, he will at the same time condemn without reserve the injustice and barbarity of those who have either secretly encouraged, or by open violence perpetrated such deeds of cruelty.

You, my friends, will, I am sure, join with me, in hoping that, if there be in this town, or in his Majesty's dominions, a wretch so entirely lost to every sense of humanity and justice as to concert this plan of villainy; or, under any pretext whatever to put it into execution—that such a miscreant may be pursued till overtaken by the vigilance of justice, and rewarded according to his foul deserts.

With these sentiments (which I am persuaded are common to my Townsmen on this occasion) you must suppose, my friends, I felt as you do, a mixture of surprise and indignation, at being told by Dr. Priestley, and in a tone of the gravest confidence too, that these outrages are to be ascribed to "the Discourses of our Teachers," (meaning, no doubt, the acting Clergy) as well as to the conduct of some of our "superiors," who are well known to have made a practice of "drinking damnation to the Dissenters," &c.

Who these our superiors are, who can allow themselves in such habits of indecency and profaneness, I profess myself very happy in

---

* An admirable Reply to this Letter has been published by Swinney and Co., Birmingham. Price 6d.

not knowing; but of the conduct of our teachers, long observation and experience, have taught me something; and to this I can speak explicitly.

I am fully aware, with you, my friends, that the present is a very delicate conjuncture, and that every precaution should be taken to allay, rather than to excite, or increase, the very unhappy resentments which the late disorders have produced. I can, at the same time, allow to the feelings of an injured man every thing that can reasonably be demanded in apology for Dr. Priestley on this occasion. Justice, however, to the character of a body of men whom their known moderation (in so critical a situation as this has been for some years past) obliges me to respect—common justice will not allow me to conceal my opinion, that the method taken by that gentleman in his address to us, is far, very far indeed, from being calculated to meliorate our present evils, or to heal our breaches.

You must be conscious, my Townsmen, that with respect to the clergy in general, the representation of their conduct given by Dr. Priestley, is in itself a calumny which no part of their practice will justify, or has in any wise provoked. If in defending their own principles, his have been occasionally glanced at, or openly attacked, we, my friends, have not considered this as necessarily, nor at all, involving an attack on Dr. Priestley's persons. We have merely looked upon our teacher as discharging a duty which, from the general integrity of their conduct, we have good reason to believe, the clear and full conviction of their consciences, strengthened by the most solemn obligations their office required them to perform. But will a conduct like this (innocent and praise-worthy as it must appear to every man who thinks the truths of religion worth contending for) justify Dr. Priestley in holding our teachers up to the world as calumniators, movers of popular tumult, and even as incendiaries! If it will not, we ask, in what light Dr. Priestley's conduct must appear in the eyes of all Europe?

Let him calmly review his Letter to the Minister—let him seriously revolve those extraordinary specimens of plain argument and perfect good temper, his Familiar Addresses to us; and before he closes the review, let him call to mind a certain *preface*, never to be forgotten, of which one of your teachers was *accidentally* the occasion; and if he must still persist in charging the late disturbances on the discourses, preached or published of individuals, we entreat him, in the presence of the great searcher of hearts, to consider, to whose discourses those public disorders are most reasonably to be ascribed, to his own, or those of our teachers.

We, who are certainly the best judges of what their conduct has been with reference to Dr. Priestley, are witnesses for them, that in whatever abhorrence they may hold some of his opinions; with regard to his person, or those of dissenters in general, the tendency of their public discourses has been in direct contradiction to the very unbecoming, and we must, in justice to our feelings, add, cruel representation given of it by Dr. Priestley. Had their conduct really been what Dr. Priestley states in his address, it could not have escaped us, that in acting thus, our teachers must not only have been guilty of misrepresenting his sentiments, but must also have shamefully forgotten their own;—these, we assure you, inculcate nothing but peace on earth and good-will to men.

Under so foul an aspersion, introduced with such artless address and simple confidence, as were most likely to obtain it credit; and thrown into such a variety of channels as were sure to give it notoriety in every part of the kingdom:—we congratulate our teachers on the consciousness they must feel in not having, in any way whatever, been accessaries* to the late melancholy disturbances.

Indeed, the known conduct of many of our clergy on the occasion, is a sufficient refutation of this injurious calumny. I myself was witness, in more than one instance, that several of them, at the risk of insult, and even personal danger, were not backward to shew their settled abhorrence of whatever has a tendency to affect the security of individuals, or to disturb the envied tranquility of their country. Dr. Priestley is undoubtedly a very great sufferer, and as such he is justly entitled to commiseration—he should however recollect, that the way to obtain that sympathy, and to secure the good opinion of his fellow citizens in general, is not by thus wantonly attacking the characters of the innocent.

AN INHABITANT.

Birmingham, July 25, 1791.

* *Sic* in original.

To the Rev. Dr. Priestley.

Quid minus utile fuit quam ulcus hoc tangere?

REV. SIR,

TO deplore the loss of your Apparatus, your Books, and Manuscripts was natural, and every Friend of Science condoles with you; to remind the deluded people that they were injuring their own cause, was just and proper. The same admonition had been given them by the laity and clergy of their own communion: but the accusation you bring against the gentlemen and the clergy, as the causes either direct or indirect of the outrages committed, is neither prudent nor true. It is not prudent, because the present moment requires the most conciliatory language; it is not true, for our warfare is not with your persons or your property, but with your opinions. As christians, you have endeavoured to deprive us of the comfortable doctrines of Atonement and Grace: as citizens, you have endeavoured to make us, like yourself, gloomy, querulous, and petulant, and though the inflammatory paper alluded to may not have been yours, the substance of it will be found in your writings.

I am, Sir, your most obedient servant,

CLERICUS.

Dr. Priestley to the Printer of the Birmingham Gazette.

SIR,

I DO not now write to complain of my sufferings in general, but of one in particular, which may in some measure be alleviated.

Private letters are a species of property peculiarly sacred. No person of honour will even look into a letter not directed to himself; and yet many of mine, I understand, are circulated, read, and detained from me, without any regard to decency or justice. A stranger picked up two that had been written to me by a late Bishop, and, instead of sending them to *me*, he sent them to the present bishop of the same See, who also, instead of sending them to me, sent them to the son of the late bishop, from whom I have just received them.

To have private letters (which are often improper to be seen by one's nearest friends) exposed to every impertinent eye, is one of the most painful circumstances in my situation. I hope, therefore, that even enemies, who have any regard to their character will send any letter of mine that may fall into their hands, sealed up, to those who will convey them to me with the least expence. There are dishonourable, as well as honourable methods, of annoying an adversary.

It may be necessary to inform some persons, that no one can detain, or destroy the property of another (and letters are property) without being subject to an action. If any private papers be sent to a Secretary of State, and he be bound by the rules of justice and honour, he will return them, or at least, copies of them, to the person whose property they are.

I am, Sir, yours, J. PRIESTLEY.

From the Committee of Dissenters.

Birmingham, Aug. 22, 1791.

WHEREAS it now appears, that amongst other insidious and unwarrantable practices made use of during the late riots, to delude the populace, and instigate them to acts of violence and destruction, letters were forged, charging the dissenters with a treasonable design to overthrow the present happy constitution of this kingdom, and pretending that the whole body of them were combined together,

and

and had appointed to assemble on the 16th of August, "to burn the churches, blow up the parliament, cut off the head of the King, and abolish all taxes:" And whereas it is now well known, that such forged letters were pretended to be found among the papers of the Rev. Dr. Priestley, and Wm. Russell, Esq., and the words above quoted formed part of one of the forged letters which were brought and read by two persons on horse-back at Showell-green, the house of Wm. Russell, Esq., whilst the same was in flames, in order to instigate the rioters to further acts of violence: Notice is hereby given, that the protestant dissenters of Birmingham, in addition to the Reward of One Hundred Pounds, graciously offered by his Majesty for discovering the instigators of the late horrid violences, will give a further reward of One Hundred Pounds for the discovery of the person or persons who wrote the said forged letters, or any one of them, so that he or they may be convicted thereof, and brought to punishment.

THOMAS LEE, jun.
Secretary to Committee of Protestant Dissenters
in Birmingham.

Temple Row, Birmingham, Saturday, July 16, 1791.

WHEREAS some detestable *villains*, from the most wicked motives, to injure Mr. WM. WINDSOR, a tenant of Mr. BROOKE's, at *Ashsted*,* have circulated a report that Mr. WINDSOR's buildings at *Ashsted*, belong to the *Corporation of Coventry*. As such report is evidently intended to incense the *friends* of CHURCH and KING, to *destroy* the property of the said WM. WINDSOR; Mr. BROOKE, whose *most* hearty attachment is *well-known* to the *real friends* of CHURCH and KING, begs leave to address them with the most solemn *assurance*, upon the *word* and *honour* of a CHURCH and KING's MAN, that the *Corporation of Coventry*, nor any *Presbyterian*, have any concern or interest whatever, in the *buildings* and property of the said Wm. WINDSOR, at *Ashsted*, nor in any of the *buildings* belonging to Mr. BROOKE, or any other person at *Ashsted*, and that upon all elections for the City of Coventry, where the said Wm. WINDSOR lived before he came to *Ashsted*, he uniformly voted *against* the *Corporation and Presbyterian interest*, and always supported the REAL TRUE BLUE, which is the CHURCH and KING party.

Mr. BROOKE therefore is convinced, that this ADDRESS will be attended to by the GENTLEMEN in the CHURCH and KING party, and hereby offers a reward of Ten Guineas, for the detection of the *rascals* who gave rise to so false a report.

Church and King for ever.†

* *Sic* in original.

† This Paper, and the two following, could not be inserted in their proper place, without interrupting the Narrative.

From the Birmingham Gazette of July 18, 1791.

Birmingham, July 16, 1791.

Friends and Fellow Countrymen,

IT is earnestly requested, that every *true friend* to the *Church of England*, and to the laws of his country, will reflect how much a *continuance* of the present proceedings must injure *that church* and *that King they are intended to support*; and how highly unlawful it is to destroy the rights and property of *any* of our neighbours. And all *true friends* to the town and trade of Birmingham, *in particular*, are intreated to forbear *immediately* from all riotous and violent proceedings; dispersing and returning peaceably to their trades and callings, as the only way to do *credit to themselves* and *their cause*, and to promote the peace, happiness, and prosperity of this great and flourishing town.

———

Birmingham, Sunday, July 17, 1791.

Important Information to the FRIENDS *of* CHURCH *and* KING.

Friends and Fellow Churchmen,

BEING convinced you are unacquainted, that the great losses which are sustained by *your burning* and *destroying* of the houses of so many individuals, will eventually fall upon the *county at large*, and not upon the persons to whom they belonged, we feel it our duty to inform you, that the damages already done, upon the best computation that can be made, will amount to upwards of *One Hundred Thousand Pounds:* the whole of which enormous sum will be charged upon the respective parishes, and paid out of the rates. We, therefore, as your *friends*, conjure you immediately to desist from the destruction of *any more houses*; otherwise the very proceedings of your *zeal* for shewing your attachment to the CHURCH and KING, will inevitably be the means of most seriously injuring innumerable families, who are hearty supporters of Government, and bring on an addition of taxes, which *yourselves, and the rest of the Friends of the Church*, will for years feel a very grievous burthen.

This we assure you was the case in London, when there were so many houses, and public buildings burnt and destroyed in the year 1780, and you may rely upon it, will be the case on the present occasion. And we must observe to you, that *any further* violent proceedings will more offend your King and Country than serve the cause of Him and the Church.

Fellow Churchmen, as you love your King, regard his laws, and restore peace.   GOD SAVE THE KING.

Aylesford	Edward Carver	Charles Curtis
E. Finch	John Brooke	Spencer Madan
Robert Lawley	J. Carles	Edward Palmer
Rob. Lawley, jun.	B. Spencer	W. Villers
R. Moland	H. Gres. Lewis	W. W. Mason
W. Digby		

Dr.

Dr. Tatham's Letter to the Dissenters.

To George Rous, Esq., President, and to the Patrons of the Anniversary of the French Revolution,

Holden at the Crown and Anchor Tavern, on the 14th of July, 1791.

AS I found it inconsistent with my honour and repugnant to my feelings, as an Englishman, to give you my personal attendance at the Crown and Anchor, I transmitted my sentiments on the occasion to *John Barker Church, Esq.*, M.P., one of the stewards, requesting that my letter might be publicly read in the Anniversary. This request, I understand, was not complied with; the reason of which I am at a loss to conjecture, unless it be that men are unwilling to be informed of their *mistakes;* or that I addressed an assembly whose principles and sentiments, both in politics and religion, are superlatively sublime, by the Gothic name of *Gentlemen*. With all proper attention and respect for so considerable a class of people, I shall, on the present occasion, change the appellation for one more appropriated to your character; and, as ye *dissent* from your fellow-citizens in political and religious tenets, or are the dupes of those who do, it will properly express you all.

By your Anniversary, ye Dissenters, and others, which ye promoted among your brethren in different parts of England, whatever was the ostensible subject, or whatever was the occasional pretence, it at length appears too plainly, that your real object was to give your democratical principles a rapid currency throughout the nation, to render Englishmen dissatisfied with their present form of Government, and to prepare the public mind for that Revolution in the State, which ye have so long, so anxiously, and so ignorantly desired; but how totally have ye mistaken both *yourselves* and *all true Englishmen?*

As to YOURSELVES, notwithstanding all the pains and assiduity ye have employed these many years, by every private and public art which the rack of ingenuity could invent, to work your sect into importance, and your tenets into practice, ye find them universally rejected and yourselves contemned. Notwithstanding all the noise and bustle ye have made with your tongues and with your pens, by your hirelings and coadjutors, in pamphlets, in newspapers, and in reviews, which for the promotion of your purpose, ye have almost entirely engrossed, all your industry has failed, and your schemes have miscarried: and ye experimentally find that the *loyalty* of Englishmen, which ye have moved every engine to subvert, is that native virtue without which they cannot exist, that sacred, deep-rooted principle which no power can shake.

Thus, however prominent your hopes, and sanguine your expectations, ye have found them totally disappointed, and yourselves neglected by every description and class of men. When the day of your anticipated triumph came, "big with the fate of Cato and Rome," which ye had announced with a proud and growing confidence, and in which your wishes were to meet their consummation in the conversion of the people—the second Anniversary of the French Revolution—what an appearance did ye make! Your very leaders, who on a former occasion, hoped to convert you into the tool of party, now considered you not worth their pains. Where were those splendid characters by whom your Anniversary was conducted a year ago? Where was *The puissant Lord* who took the chair on the 14th of July, 1790, and presided with the intrepidity of a lion elected King! Was he gone to claim a seat among the enlightened patriots of the neighbouring continent, whom he so much admired. May his political principles and conduct receive their merited reward in the Congress of America, or in the National Assembly of France, instead of the British House of Peers! Where was *The Man of the People*, as he is falsely called, that consummate general in politics, who with equal dexterity can employ his shafts on every side? Was he gone to seek another coalition with a Minister of State?—May every British Minister reflect with horror on the disgrace and ruin of the last, and shun him as a precipice! Where was *The Friend and Patron of the Comic Muse*, that champion of false liberty, bold in his flight, and soaring as an eagle? Was his boldness suppressed and his pinions shackled by the injunction of an illustrious Prince, who excels him as much in sterling understanding as he does in native dignity? May that illustrious Prince employ that understanding on all other occasions, and discard from his person and councils, as the worst of sycophants, all who are hostile to the crown and constitution of England! *One of your Apostles of Liberty* is gone before to reap the fruits of his political labours. May his mistakes be pardoned, his errors cancelled, and his Manes rest in peace! But where was that *other Apostle of ideal Liberty*, who still survives? Was he more usefully employed in patronising another Anniversary at Birmingham, where, for eleven years, he has been propagating his more than apostolical doctrine against the Church and King of England!—Alas! I shudder whilst I relate. Kindled with a spark of that loyalty which nothing can extinguish in the breasts of Englishmen, the populace revolted against their pastor, and, in the paroxism of a tumultuous and ungoverned zeal, have committed outrages, which, whilst he applauds the motive, every Englishman must lament. May he live to repent of the injuries he has done his country and mankind, in more respects than one; and instead of prevaricating and perverting scripture in a letter of exculpation, let him attribute to himself and the Anniversary the *sole cause* of the riot and devastation that ensued.

And ye have not only mistaken yourselves and been deserted by your

your leaders; ye have mistaken ALL TRUE ENGLISHMEN. With the learned and the wise, who must ever be the few, your political sophistry has produced no effect or emotion but contempt. With the simple and the ignorant, who must always be the many, your hopes were placed. But, however simple and ignorant, they are sensible of their happinesss, and independent in their spirit; and they have given you a tremendous proof that they possess the hearts and prejudices of Englishmen, which no sophistry can pervert or change. In this crown and summit of your expectation, in which your meditated Revolution was to find its origin, how universally are ye disappointed? The common people of England (and when I speak of England I speak of Britain) whom ye have so much studied, and courted with such assiduity, ye did not understand. They are as loyal as they are brave, and brave as loyal. No sooner did they see through the artful veil, which ye throw over everything ye say or do, to the end ye have in view, the disturbance of their national peace and happiness in Church and State, and an attempt upon the Government under which these blessings are enjoyed, than that common people, whom ye thought ye had moulded to your purpose, felt themselves injured and insulted; and their resentment, when it took fire, has proved as severe as it was honest.

Thus, ye Dissenters, *ye have mistaken altogether*, and are at length convinced, if facts and experience can convince you, that *your mistake has involved in its consequences*, as I admonished you before, *much public and private evil*, and was in danger of involving more.

Ye are dissatisfied and deluded men, who, seeing licentiousness and low ambition under the mask of liberty, laying waste a neighbouring kingdom, and erecting on its ruins the worst of tyranny, are eager to emulate its phrenzy, by stimulating your country to imitate its example. Your Anniversary and the *Toasts* ye drank at London, as well as they at Birmingham, and have had the audacity to publish, proclaim to the world this infatuated truth. Your toasts are replete with faction and disaffection, which were artfully intended to be the more effective by being mixed with what wears the face, but only the face, of loyalty. Instead of being the *friends of liberty in England*, as in your invitation ye pretended, however ye may shuffle and prevaricate in words (for the whole of your conduct is made up of artifice and evasion) your toasts and actions have made it *plain that ye wish to effect*, as I informed you, *the public affairs and local concerns of this country*, in total destruction of that liberty, and to plunge England into the anarchy and misery of France.

Your first toast, *The Rights of Men*, is a phantom conjured up among the French and among yourselves, the disciples of a visionary and chimerical philosophy, as the basis of all your political fabrications, without a correspondent reality in the world;

which

which, however, it may stimulate an infatuated race to pull down the civil power, can never assist them to build another.

In the second, ye drank *The Nation, the Law, and the King;* and what sort of King ye meant is obvious from the third, in which ye celebrated your favourite subject, *The Revolution of France;* and also from the seventh, in which ye drank, *The Sovereignty of the People.* It is clear from hence, that ye did not mean such a King as *George the Third,* the sovereign Monarch of Great Britain, but as *Louis the Sixteenth,* the present King, or rather prisoner, of the French. And as to the *nation* and the *law,* ye surely neither understood the constitution of the one, nor the spirit and letter of the other; for history and experience have informed us, that the *constitution* of Great Britain cannot subsist without a King, vested with that plentitude of regal power possessed by George the Third; that *such a King* cannot exist in that constitution without his *church,* his *nobles,* and his faithful *commons;* all which principalities and powers are established, confirmed, and sanctioned by the whole authority of the *law.* When, in the eighth toast, ye celebrated *perfect liberty,* with much apparent zeal, ye knew not what it is: for without such a law there can exist no *British liberty,* the *most perfect* of all other; and without such a King that law can have *no effect.* If, therefore, ye understood the nature of true liberty and public happiness, which are synonymous, ye would be thankful, in the first place, that the *nation* has such a *law* and such a *king* as those of England; and, in the second, that that king is *George the Third;* for, however, ye may affect to hold him cheap, as the French (whom in all things ye wish to imitate) do Louis XVI., he possesses as much sound understanding as the wisest of you all, more true piety than the most sanctified of you all, and more honesty than ye altogether.

Your triumph in the ninth toast, over Mr. Burke, who so ably rang the fire bell of your sedition, is the emptiest gasconade, by which ye have shewn yourselves *Frenchmen* in manners as well as sentiment. Neither Mr. Burke, nor the other friends of the British Government, will shrink from the political discussion in which ye so vainly glory, when sound reasoning and sound principles are employed: but they cannot be expected to stoop to the notice of the ignorant and audacious ribaldry of Mr. *Paine.* Your *two Apostles of Liberty* are your ablest champions, and they have been refuted without an answer: for, however you may toast *the free principles of the British Constitution,* and they may have written on the *Principles of Government* in general, they are as totally ignorant of the one, as ye have shewn yourselves unacquainted with the other.

Was it loyal or respectful to that King and Government, under whose auspicies ye enjoy more liberty than ye deserve, to insult them openly by the names of *Washington* and *Franklin,* the arch-rebel and arch-traitor of Old England, and to celebrate in a toast of joy,

joy, the *disjunction of America* from the British Crown? Ye might have been content in having privately encouraged and fomented the first unnatural rebellion, in privately rejoicing together at the defeat of a Cornwallis, and in weeping together over that of a Montgomery, and in privately triumphing in your own disgrace, without offering on the high altar of sedition, formerly erected for the purpose in your Anniversary, a public insult to your King and country.

Did not this, in addition to your disaffected conduct, and as the crown to your disloyalty, strongly savour of " Faction tending to the disturbance of the public peace*;" and of "Rebellious riot and tumult, to the disturbance of the public peace, and to the endangering of his Majesty's person and government, fomented by persons disaffected to his Majesty, by which his Majesty and his administration hath been most maliciously and falsely traduced, with intent to raise divisions, and to alienate the affections of his people from his Majesty †?"

Thus, ye Dissenters, by your anniversaries at London, and elsewhere, ye have shewn yourselves disaffected to our present happy government in church and state, and anxious to change it for one infinitely worse; and ye have hereby proved yourselves, as I foretold, *an example of the operation of the French Revolution, in disturbing the peace and tranquility of England*: for a conduct so factious and seditious could not escape the resentment of your fellow citizens, who are loyal subjects, however patient they may be. Though prevented in London, by the vigilance of a wise and able government, ye see the effects of your anniversaries, which ye might have forseen, in the ravage and devastation of a distant county, for which, as the *sole and adequate cause*, ye and your associates at Birmingham are *accountable*. In that town and neighbourhood they have had a foretaste of that liberty resulting from an English democracy, *the sovereignty of the people*, in which ye glory: and, if your system of politics was adopted in Great Britain, the same ravage and devastation would soon be co-extensive with the island.

And now, ye Dissenters, convinced of your ignorance and *mistakes*, by that experience, which alone can make some men wise, ye will not, I hope, renew your anniversaries another year, of the *illegality* of which I had forwarned you; and which is now evinced both in your own seditious conduct, and in the riot and tumult they have occasioned. Instead of this vain testimony of such tumultuous and expensive joy for a thing ye do not understand, and with which ye have not the least concern, let me exhort you, another year, to remain peaceably and industriously at home: for if ye should attempt another such anniversary, instead of a second monitory

---

* See Bacon's Abridgment of the Law of England, vol. 3. page 37.

† 1 George I. Stat. 2. chap. 5. § 1.

letter, I will call upon the public magistrate, and take care the call shall be obeyed, to put in use the 1st Geo. I. Stat. 2. chap. 5.

In the meantime, ye Dissenters, think *soberly* and *modestly* of YOURSELVES, as ye ought to think; and *honourably* and *respectfully* of your fellow-citizens, who are TRUE ENGLISHMEN. Suppose not that ye are *better* or *wiser* than they; for this false estimate is the great root of your mistakes. Be thankful to Providence for the king that reigns over you, who is to you both a *father* and a *friend*, and for the religious liberty with which ye are so *graciously indulged*, and permit me, in return for the printed string of *toasts* lately sent me by the post, to give you one of my own, much better than them all—in defiance of your arts and machinations against them,

MAY CHURCH AND KING REMAIN FOR EVER!

I am, ye Dissenters, with deep concern for the effects of your delusion, your friend and fellow-citizen,

EDWARD TATHAM.

Bodleian Oxford,
3d of August, 1791.

The Address of GEORGE ROUS, *Esq., Chairman at the late Anniversary of the French Revolution, at the Crown and Anchor, Tavern, London, to the Public.*

MUCH industry has been employed to represent, as the enemies of public order, all those who, on the 14th of July, professed openly to rejoice at the emancipation of twenty-five millions of fellow-creatures from the yoke of despotism: who hailed, with exultation, the generous and beneficent (even as if it were visionary) attempt to realize those rights, which all theorists have acknowledged to be the result of moral reasoning, the legitimate source of human laws; and the protection of which constitutes the sole object of all just Government. The calumnies directed against myself will not provoke reply; but I cannot resist my inclination to point the public attention to the *opposite* effects which have naturally followed from the *opposite* principles of the two parties.

Those men *must* be the friends of peace, whose fixed principles require them to claim no rights for themselves, which they are not equally ready to maintain for others—to wish that the voice of truth only may be heard—and to effect no change which shall not be previously sanctioned by the consenting reason of mankind. Accordingly, in the numerous places where the French Revolution has been celebrated by convivial meetings, no symptoms of ill-will to any human being has appeared among its friends. In Birmingham alone the cry of Church and King has resounded, and a disciplined banditti, professing *to obey orders*, have destroyed the houses of Revolutionists and Anti-revolutionists, of the friends and enemies of the present Ministers

Ministers with the most impartial outrage. The sole pretext has been, the men presumed to worship God in the manner they deemed most acceptable to the divine nature. The miserable deluded wretches, the immediate instruments of violence, who must now be sacrificed to the laws of their country, can excite compassion alone. Thinking men will endeavour to eradicate the source of this evil. When governors punish imputed error as convicted guilt, and mark men as a distinct race for a difference of opinion, on a subject where the most unlimited exercise of private judgment is duty,—when a Right Rev. Prelate, in the plenitude of his charity, denounces, as unworthy sons of the Church, those meek Christians who shall presume even to vote for a Member of parliament, *profane* enough to believe that *supposed error* ought not to be treated as a *crime*, or punished by proscription from the common rights of citizenship,—when Tests, as an elegant author expresses it, "profane the rights of religion they pretend to guard, and usurp the dominion of the God they pretend to revere,"—is it wonderful that the untaught multitude should believe the interests of Church and King may be advanced by conflagrations lighted in the houses of their fellow-citizens?

I can differ from Dr. Priestley without feeling the smallest diminution of that esteem which his talents and virtues have impressed. After reading his arguments, I retain a firm conviction that a precarious provision for the Clergy has a tendency to degrade religion in the person of its Ministers; though truth compels me to acknowledge, that the teachers of dissenting congregations in this kingdom form a splendid exception to the general rule. But the zeal of dissent, with other causes, may operate an effect scarcely to be expected in the absence of these motives; and it is safe, at least, to place the Clergy of the national religion in a state, whenever they deserve, to command respect. Yet a hint may not be useless to the zealots of our Church, that a subversion in Civil Government of the first principles of justice, by an ignominious exclusion of great bodies of our fellow-citizens from political trusts, is not the best possible mode of protecting establishments from the inquisitive spirit of an enlightened age.

GEO. ROUS.

Lincoln's-inn Fields, July 24, 1791.

From the Morning Chronicle of July 28, 1791.

To the Editor.

SIR,

IN some ministerial Papers, the Dissenters have been represented as in a state of despondency and dejection, in consequence of the sufferings of their brethren at Birmingham. As far as my acquaintance

acquaintance with Dissenters extends, I know not a single instance to verify this observation, that has been made with so much triumph and complacency. That this has not been the case with any individual among them, I will not presume to affirm, for in all great bodies there are timid men to be met with; but that they have no cause for despondency or dejection of any kind, it is very easy to shew.

The simple fact is this, that some Dissenters of great eminence, and of acknowledged worth of character, have had their houses destroyed, their property plundered, and their lives put into imminent danger, by a furious mob, who have been called the friends of the King, and of the Church of England.

Let us now examine into the crimes which led those friends of the King, and of the Church of England, to adopt such violent measures. The charge alledged,* is disaffection to our Constitution in Church and State.

Whether this charge be or be not well founded, it happens to have been advanced at a time and place extremely ill chosen, with respect to those who have brought it forward; at a time when Dissenters, together with Members of the Church of England, had been drinking the King and Constitution as a toast; at a meeting held in a room that had been ornamented with an emblem, expressive of very warm loyalty, and at which a gentleman of respectability presided, well known in the world of science and of letters, and moreover a Member of the Church of England. It is plain then, that there was nothing in the celebration of the anniversary of the taking of the Bastille, and of the origin of French Liberty, to furnish even a pretext for the outrages that have been committed.

We must suppose then that the charge was founded on other grounds, to which the Loyalists and Churchmen of Birmingham, who stood forth the active champions of their principles on the late occasion, must have been entire strangers, had not they been stated to them, by others better acquainted with these matters than themselves.

We will suppose then, that the offence arose from the writings of certain Dissenters; writings in which they shew themselves to be disaffected to our Constitution in Church and State. Admitting this to be notoriously the case, I would beg leave to ask some furious persons, whether, after cool reflection, they think that a mob ought to be let loose upon them, to abuse their persons, to burn their houses, and to plunder their property. Can the spirit of Englishmen be reconciled—can the laws of the country be made to comport with so savage a mode of punishment? The sense of every unbiassed person revolts at the idea—there lives not an honest man that shudders not at the thought—there is not a nation than ranks among those called civilized, even where bigotry reigns most triumphant, that would incur the disgrace of sanctioning such a procedure, as that carried on by those very indecently called the friends of the Church at Birmingham.

It

* Sic in original.

It were better to be dragooned, as the Protestants were in France, in the reign of Louis XIV. at the time of the revocation of the edict at Nantes, than to be committed into the hands of a drunken populace. If it should be thought right to have this measure followed by others of a similar nature, I hope such friends of the King and of the Church will give timely notice of their intentions, that Dissenters, if they are constrained to leave their property behind, may at least carry away their persons unhurt, to some more benignant climes, where the iron hand of intolerance is not felt. This surely will not be deemed too great a boon to give them. Worthy Churchmen may be offended at any one's making such a supposition, I do not mean it for them, but solely for those who have entered so deeply into the spirit of party, as to have lost all sense of candour, and even of common justice.

But let us see how the Dissenters stand with regard to the charge that has above been stated. Many Dissenters are of opinion, that our civil constitution is extremely corrupt, and that it needs to be reformed. Is this opinion peculiar to Dissenters? Are there not within the pale of the Church, names the most revered, who have distinguished themselves by their zeal for this very opinion? Has any man, Churchman or Dissenter, expressed himself more strongly upon this subject, than the present Minister of this Country? Did he not promise to support measures for a Parliamentary Reform, both as a man and a Minister? If the Dissenters are wrong in this matter, and if Churchmen, among whom may be named the late Sir George Savile, Mr. Fox, Major Cartwright, Mr. Wyvil, and a host besides, of all that is great and respectable, with the Prime Minister at their head, have been, and still are wrong in this matter, why are the Dissenters alone to bear the blame? If the measure be right, and should hereafter happen to be adopted, posterity will, I am sure, not allow them all the merit of it; if it be not a right measure, why should any fear that the discerning spirit of the impartial public will not discover its ill tendency. If court favours, and all that is most flattering to ambition and vanity, be sufficient to induce men of talents to point out its fallacy, there will not be wanting those who will engage in the work. If there be any thing in endeavours to awaken the sense of Englishmen, to demand a more equal representation of the people in Parliament, that militates against the peace and order of society, why is not the full force of the law applied to prevent it?— Why has not a statute, enforced by proper penalties, been passed for that purpose, for the evil, if it be one, has been of long duration?

On the discussions to which the Revolutions in France have given occasion, I should have blushed for the Dissenters, if none of them had stood forth to defend the common cause. Besides Doctors Priestley and Towers, Mr. Lofft, Mr. Christie, the Country Attorney, and the Country Justice of Peace, I know of none among the

Dissenters who entered the lists. They cannot claim the honour of reckoning among their body the other numerous answerers of Mr. Burke, Earl Stanhope, Geo. Rous, Esq., Sir Brook Boothby, Mrs. Macaulay Graham, Mrs. Wollstonecraft, Mr. Mackintosh, and Thomas Paine, it is well known, are not Dissenters. I would ask, in the language of our adversaries, were the Dissenting writers the most intemperate of those that appeared in this controversy? But there are among the Dissenters warm admirers of Mr. Paine? are there not more in the Church who prize his work as highly? Why then, in the name of all that is fair and equitable, is the whole blame to be thrown upon one set of people, who, if they are in an error, share it in common with some of their most respectable neighbours? Let then the friends of the Church of England bring all the members of that Church into a right mind upon the subject, before they burn the places of worship, and plunder the property of the Dissenters. If there is a want of candour in the strictures made by these writers upon the Constitution, the Dissenters can urge pleas which Churchmen cannot; the civil disabilities under which this Constitution places them, forms a stigma, which, as men of honour, they cannot help deeply feeling.

It is farther said, that the Dissenters are disaffected to the Church. If by that is meant, that they do not believe all its doctrines, nor approve of all its rites and ceremonies, and form of government, there is clearly no warding off the charge. If it be a crime to be disaffected to the Church, it is a crime to be a Dissenter, and the law of England not only tolerates crimes, but protects English subjects in the exercise of what is criminal. But that the English government does not regard any religious opinions as criminal, is apparent from its having established Popery in Quebec, Presbyterianism in Scotland, and Episcopacy in England. Many Dissenters are of opinion, that there is no necessary connexion between Church and State; that such an alliance (as it has been called) is injurious to both. The Church, they apprehend, they can prove to be very capable of being employed, in the hands of the executive power, to the detriment of the rights and liberties of the people. They also apprehend, that the best ends which religion, even in a political view, can answer, are defeated, in a great degree, by a connexion with the State. To this cause they attribute that secularizing spirit, which is so notorious among the high orders of Ecclesiastics, and which is so hostile to that spirit of piety and humility by which they ought to be distinguished. These are sentiments, no doubt, highly disagreeable to numbers of persons, but they are the honest convictions of many Dissenters: convictions to which they were led by inquiries, suggested to them by the situations in which they find themselves as Dissenters. They do not regard them as uninteresting speculations, but as subjects of importance, highly worthy of

being

being discussed. They have not attempted to propagate them in an underhand way, but they have openly published them to the world, and left them to stand or fall, to spread, or to sink into oblivion, according as they should appear to be true or false. The opponents of those principles have not always shewn that confidence in the inherent excellence of their cause, which those who are unfriendly to them could wish they had done. The only guilt then that falls upon Dissenters, is that of discussing these points. If discussion ought not to be tolerated, why are not laws enacted, enjoining the prohibition of it? Why do we profess that these are times, those happy times, to which the words of the Roman Historian are applicable: "*Ubi sentire quæ velis et quæ sentias dicere licet.*" Freedom of discussion being universally supposed to be the privilege of Britons, a weapon with which every one who knew how to wield it might securely attack, whatever appeared to him to be corrupt or radically wrong in Church or State.

This having been the conduct of Dissenters, they cannot see that they have incurred any blame; they sympathize, but do not despond. Those of them who have suffered in the present instance, do not supplicate, but claim, with as much confidence as any other order of citizens, the protection of the laws, and demand a reparation of their injuries.

Those who have most reason for lamentation in the present instance, are the friends of the Church of England, on account of the misguided and ferocious zeal of their brethren, who have disgraced their cause, by using antichristian weapons, and by committing outrages which, whenever they are mentioned, will make every ingenuous Churchman blush.

The Dissenters have the feelings of those whose friends have been robbed and plundered; the friends of the Church of England, if they acknowledge the rioters at Birmingham as Fellow-churchmen, must feel as those do whose brethren have been guilty of those flagrant acts of injustice, which the laws of their country decree deserving of being punished capitally. I do not mean to say, that the upright Churchman, who is tolerant in his principles and practice, is to be charged with a single particle of the guilt of his persecuting Fellow-churchmen, who will answer for their conduct at the tribunal of their country. Those only participate in the guilt of these practices who abet them. Which then have cause to appear dejected? the plundered and their friends, or the plunderers and those who are united to them by the ties of religious profession? I leave the question to be answered by every unbiassed person.

I will state the case wherein the Dissenters would have appeared to despond; the present is not that case. Had any of their communion instigated mobs to demolish churches; had they set them upon attempts to insult and plunder the most revered for amiableness of manners, and brilliancy of talents, and the most distinguished, by just celebrity, of the champions of the Church; had they burned the houses, pillaged the property, and ransacked the private concerns of the most respectable of its commercial members, then indeed would the Dissenters have held down their heads ashamed and abashed, and they would have had cause for so doing. Had any of their persuasion outraged the meanest Ecclesiastic, I am well aware, that the Dissenters would, to a man, have felt honest shame for the unworthy behaviour of such persons.

Should any presume, that in consequence of what has happened, we shall be less open and spirited in the avowal of our religious and political principles than we have hitherto been, they are most assuredly mistaken. Rational sentiments in religion, and political doctrines founded on the rights of men, will prevail, whatever becomes of Dissenters. Were the Dissenters all banished the kingdom, there is no doubt but that there would start up, out of the bosom of the Church of England, men in abundance to support those religious and political principles, the odium of which it seems to be now the policy to throw upon Dissenters. Yet it will not be imagined that such ungenerous methods, as those are, which have been practised at Birmingham, will prove any permanent injury to the principles which Dissenters hold, or ever prevent Dissenters from asserting or defending them. If the principles are well founded, a repetition of the fires of Smithfield will be insufficient to crush them; if they are false, the discussion which their advocates provoke will prove fatal to them.

I am, Sir, Yours, &c.,

A DISSENTER.

EXTRACT FROM THE
Preface to the Rev. Mr. Scholefield's Sermon,*

Preached to the two Congregations of the Old and New Meetings, on their first assembling after the destruction of those places, from Matt. v. 44, "But I say unto you, love your enemies, bless them that curse "you, do good to them that hate you, and pray for them which des- "pitefully use you, and persecute you."

"SHOULD this Discourse fall into the hands of any of the enemies to the Dissenters (for enemies undoubtedly they have) it may lead them, through the divine blessing, to the most serious reflexions upon the atrociousness of their late conduct.

"If such are the directions of *Christ*, in respect to enemies, how much more ought they to feel their own departure from the benevo-

Printed by Belcher, Birmingham, price 1s.

lent spirit of Christianity, in the violence and animosity exercised against those from whom they have never received any real injury. Severe, indeed, must be their reflexions, if ever they are brought to take a serious and impartial review of the evils and calamities they have occasioned.—How black is the list which recollection places before them!

"They have burnt down, with unprovoked rage and fury, two of the largest and most respectable places of worship, amongst the Dissenters, in this kidgdom;—they have levelled with the ground, or ravaged, the houses of as valuable, peaceful citizens, as this country can boast;—they have destroyed the habitation, and banished (for the present) from his friends and family, a Man, who, for temper, abilities, and real worth, is an *ornament* to human nature; who has been admired and distinguished by every friend to literature, and whom foreign nations would esteem it an *honour* to have enrolled among them.—In fine, they have stained the future annals of our country with instances of rapine, injustice, and violence, to which its previous history, for centuries past, can scarce afford a parallel.

"The Author, at the time, was at a distance from home, and only learnt, in general, that it was the act of an undistinguished mob:—but great was his surprize, and equal his indignation, to find on his return, not like St. Paul when walking through the streets of Athens, an inscription *to an unknown God;* but an appeal to *two* sources of Authority, which ought to have been treated with higher respect, either as a willing or forced vindication of their conduct—CHURCH and KING appeared wrote upon every house; and the *actors* in the scene claimed the honour of being their most *steady* and *zealous defenders.*

"His Majesty has, with a zeal and speed suited to a *parental care*, shown his marked disapprobation of *such defenders*, by sending immediate relief, and publishing his royal proclamation. Numbers, likewise, of the Established Church, have, as individuals, acted a most *friendly* and *benevolent* part; but general reflexions or charges, upon large and public bodies of men, require as public and extensive a refutal.

"Truly concerned for the honour of a Church, with whose officiating Clergy he held the most intimate and friendly intercourse, for the first seventeen years of his own public ministry; a Church from particular members of which he has received many proofs and instances of marked and distinguished respect and kindness; the author has waited, with a friendly impatience to see a public Meeting of its Clergy and Laity called, and as public a disavowal and abhorrence of the late riotous measures (ostensibly exerted in their support) expressed. Hitherto he has waited in vain; but was he allowed to argue the case with them, and was even a member of their own body, he should say until this is done, in the most open and unreserved manner, a lasting stain will remain upon the body at large. Every thinking mind will soon discover, that if the Church stands in need of such defenders—it is *weak;* if the Church approves, or even does not, in the most explicit terms, condemn them—it is *wicked.*

"Had any of the Churches of the Establishment been burnt by accident, or through age required being pulled down and re-built, the Dissenters (if necessary) would, even before this time, have furnished them with every accommodation in their power.* And shall not one expression of condolence and sympathy come from a body, under whose apparent auspices, at least, the whole of this *horrid business* has been transacted!

"He would further venture to forewarn them, without any gift of prophecy, that except a measure of this kind is adopted, many of the wiser, more moderate, and thinking part of the Church, will be inclined for ever to leave its communion. Persecution, in the darkest ages of the Church, wore always an unfriendly aspect to its interest; but the very idea of it (with the light which has now diffused itself through Europe) will strike many individuals with horror."

Copy of a Letter from M. Condorcet, *Secretary to the Academy of Sciences at Paris, to* Dr. Priestley.

Paris, *July* 30, 1791.

Sir, and most illustrious Associate,

THE Academy of Sciences have charged me to express the grief with which they are penetrated at the recital of the persecution of which you have been lately the victim.

They all feel how much loss the Sciences have experienced by the destruction of those labours which you had prepared for their aggrandisement. It is not you, Sir, who have reason to complain; your virtue and your genius still remain undiminished, and it is not in the power of human ingratitude to forget what you have done for the happiness of mankind:—they only ought to be unhappy, whose guilty conduct has led their reason astray, and whose remorse has already punished their crimes.

You are not the first friend of Liberty, against whom Tyrants have armed the very people whom they have deprived of their rights. These are the only means which they can make use of against him, whose disinterestedness of mind, whose elevation of

---

* "At Banbury (while the Chnrch is rebuilding) the Dissenters have offered the use of their Meeting to the Members of the Establishment; it has been accepted, and the Author is informed they attend public service in it at this day."

soul, and whose purity of conduct, equally shelter him from their seductions and their vengeance.

They calumniate such a person when they can neither intimidate nor corrupt him; they arm prejudices against him, when they dare not arm the laws; and that which they have done in regard to you, is the noblest homage that Tyranny dares to render to probity, to talents, and to courage.

At this present moment a league is formed throughout Europe against the general liberty of mankind; but for some time past another has existed, occupied with propagating and with defending this liberty, without any other arms than those furnished by reason; and these will finally triumph.

It is in the necessary order of things that error should be momentary, and truth eternal. Men of genius, supported by their virtuous disciples, when placed in the balance against the vulgar mob of corrupt intriguers—the instruments or the accomplices of Tyrants—must at length prevail against them. The glorious day of Universal Liberty will shine upon our descendants, but we shall at least enjoy the *aurora;* and you, Sir, have contributed not a little to accelerate that happy event by your labours, by the example of your virtues, by the indignation which all Europe feels against your persecutors, and by the interest and the admiration which a misfortune has excited, that, although it may wound, cannot subdue your soul.

I am, with an inviolable and respectful attachment,

Sir, and my very illustrious associate,

Your humble and most obedient servant,

CONDORCET.

Dr. Priestley's Answer.

SIR,

I AM more than consoled for my losses, by learning that the Members of the Academy of Sciences have honoured me, by interesting themselves in what has befallen me; and particularly as as I thereby discover, that the Friends of Philosophy are what they ever should be—the Friends of Universal Liberty. For myself, I have proved that the enemies of the one are also the enemies of the other.

Having ever been the declared advocate for public Liberty, as well civil as religious, I naturally defended by my writings your last and glorious revolution. The great body of the clergy of this country, and many of those who call themselves the King's Friends, have long been my enemies; and in their destruction of all I possessed,

possessed, they have not spared the instruments of that science, the pursuit of which has given weight to my labours of another kind.

But do not think, Sir, that these friends of the clergy and of the King compose the English nation—they belong only to a despairing faction, routed in the contest of reasoning. The sober and sensible part of the nation disapproves equally of the tenets of these factious men, and the means they employ to give them force. The English nation respects in general the French; and though at the present period too many are under error on her acconnt, yet that nation will rival yours in every thing truly grand; in all things contributive to internal honour and felicity, and in that which may be productive of peace and benevolence reciprocally with her neighbours;—but more particularly with you, who will be ever dear to us, from the generous efforts you have made in favour of universal liberty—universal peace.

I beg you will assure those who number me among themselves, and generously sympathize with my misfortunes, that so long as nature shall accord to me ability and life, I will pursue my philosophic labours—demonstrating to our common enemies, that the true love of liberty and science is extinguished but with life; and that unreasonable and wicked persecution, tends rather to animate than repress the courage of the truly enamoured. Fully convinced that what is true and just will prevail sooner or later, and that every sort of opposition, serves only the more completely to establish it,

I am, with much respect, &c.   J. PRIESTLEY.

Address of the Society of Friends of the Constitution, sitting at the Jacobins, *to* Dr. Priestley.

SIR,

MANY learned Societies have already offered you, and will yet offer you, the tribute of their sensibility on the loss which Science has suffered by the attack made on your property in its most precious particular, your Cabinet and Manuscripts. In times less troublesome, this loss, afflicting to all classes of men, would even have affected many of those who have now had the cruelty to rejoice in it, and who have entertained against your political principles a hatred which perhaps they do not feel towards you personally. You are the victim of the interest which you have taken in the cause of human nature, triumphant in the greatest Revolution which ever occurred among men. You have interrupted the course of your labours and discoveries in physics, to justify the French nation against the absurd charges brought against them, and multiplied by their oppressors, who are driven from a land of liberty. The cries of their despair, their exaggerated reproaches, their calumnious imputations, had, for a moment, spread delusion over neighbouring nations. They desired to interpose between

them

them and France a cloud which in passing, should obscure, if not totally conceal from their view the glory of the French Revolution. You, Sir, penetrated this cloud, and drew from it some sparks of light, which since have not ceased to illuminate the nations. One of your writings has victoriously repulsed the attack of one of our most unjust detractors. From this, your name, already dear in Europe to all those who cultivate the arts, or who improve their reason, becomes peculiarly dear to Frenchmen. The Society of the Friends of the Constitution were able to reckon one friend more; and recently, on the news of the misfortune which has happened to the Sciences and to the world, more than to yourself, they united with zeal and affection an emotion of indignation against those who excited the criminal attack, already punished by the noble and touching Letter which you addressed to your Fellow-citizens, and which, without doubt, is expiated in part by the remorse of most of them. The ignorance of the people is the patrimony of tyrants—but it ceases—repentance succeeds, and presently it chastises, on the heads of those who instigate to crimes, the crime of drawing forth popular delusion. The victim foresees the instant of vengeance, without permitting himself to hasten it. He consoles himself in seeing the diffusion through his country and through Europe of the generous principles of sociability, the power of which, every day augmented, is manifested in the innumerable testimonies of an universal interest in his calamity. We believe, Sir, that we enter into the secret of your character, in persuading ourselves that it is under this point of view alone, that these testimonies of an affecting esteem cannot be indifferent to you. They are proofs of the progress of these social ideas—of the public spirit which calls a free people to the practice of the virtues requisite to the maintenance of liberty, which, strengthening at home, concurs in spreading it around, and even perhaps in perfecting it among those nations who enjoyed but an incomplete freedom. In fine, these testimonies announce the developement of that philanthropic patriotism which regards all men as *in solido* associated in the common interest of general felicity; an idea so superior to the conceptions of despots and slaves, as to be the object of their contemptible derision, but which posterity will bless, as the happy fruit of that philosophy, too modern, which reckons the illustrious PRIESTLEY among its most ardent propagators. We are, &c.

Letter from the Committee *of the* Revolution Society *to* Dr. Priestley.

Reverend Sir,   August 16, 1791.

WE embrace the opportunity of the first Meeting of the Committee of the Revolution Society, subsequent to the atrocious riots which have taken place at Birmingham, to express our concern and regret at those acts of lawless violence, by which you have been so great a sufferer, and which have reflected such extreme dishonour on this age, and on this nation.

It might have been presumed, that the most ignorant and lawless savages would not have been induced to commit such depredations on the house and property of a man of such distinguished merit as yourself, to whom the whole scientific world has been so eminently indebted, and in whose works those principles of equal Liberty have been asserted and maintained, which would protect even the lowest of the human species from violence and oppression.—As a political writer, you have been employed in disseminating the most just and rational sentiments of Government, and such as are in a very high degree calculated to promote general freedom and happiness.

The conduct of the Birmingham Rioters implied in it a complication of ignorance and brutality; which it is astonishing to find at the present period in such a country as Great Britain. Nothing but the most execrable bigotry, united to ignorance the most contemptible, could lead any body of men to suppose that such acts of violence as were lately exercised at Birmingham against yourself, and other respectable Dissenters in that town and its neighbourhood, could be justified by any difference of opinion. We hoped, that the age had been more enlightened, that it had been more universally admitted, that *no* country can be possessed of freedom, in which every man is not allowed to worship God according to the dictates of his own conscience, and in which he is not permitted to defend his opinions. We hoped also, that the principles of Civil Liberty had been so well understood, and so extensively adopted, that few would have been found in this country, who would not sincerely have rejoiced at the emancipation of a neighbouring kingdom from tyranny, and in such events as are calculated to promote general liberty and happiness.

It is with exultation and triumph that we see the success of the late just, necessary, and glorious Revolution in France; an event so pregnant with the most important benefits to the world, that not to rejoice in it would be unworthy of us as Freemen, and as friends to the general rights of human nature; and to ascribe to the commemoration of the French Revolution the late devastations committed at Birmingham, would be to insult the understandings of mankind.

We are sorry to find that so many of our countrymen still need to be instructed in the first principles of civil and religious freedom. But we still hope that the period is not far distant, when the common rights of mankind will be universally acknowledged—when civil and ecclesiastical tyranny shall be banished from the face of the earth, and when it will not be found practicable to procure any licentious mobs, to support the cause of an ignorant and interested intolerance.

We again express our deep concern at the iniquitous riots which have lately happened at Birmingham, at the acts of violence and injustice

justice which have been exercised against you and your friends; and the loss science and literature have sustained in the destruction of your books, manuscripts, and philosophical apparatus.

We rejoice in the security of your person, notwithstanding the malevolence of your adversaries, and at the magnanimity with which you have sustained the injuries that you have received.

Permit us to intreat you to convey our cordial and affectionate condolence to your fellow-sufferers in the cause of freedom and public virtue—As to yourself, we desire to testify in the most public manner the high sense we entertain of your merit, and we beg leave to subscribe ourselves, with great respect and regard, Reverend Sir,

Your most obedient, and most humble servants, &c.

Declaration of the Volunteers, *and* Inhabitants at large, *of the Town and Neighbourhood of* Belfast.
July 14, 1791.

NEITHER on Marble nor on Brass can the rights and duties of Men be so durably registered, as on their memories, and on their hearts. We, therefore, meet this day to commemorate the *French Revolution*, that the remembrance of this great event may sink deeply into our hearts, warmed not merely with the fellowing-feeling* of Townsmen, but with a sympathy which binds us to the human race, in a brotherhood of Interest, of Duty, and of Affection.

A Revolution of such moment to mankind, involving so many millions, embracing so great a country, and compleated* in so short a time, is apt to confound and perplex by the magnitude of the object, and the rapidity of its motion. We, therefore, think it best to attach our minds upon one simple sublime truth, where our opinions may centre, and our judgments find stability. We are men of plain, and we hope sound understandings—We will disentangle ourselves from those bewitching bonds with which an enticing and meretricious eloquence has of late vainly endeavoured to tie down the Freedom and the Strength of Manhood; and neither sophisticated by genius, nor rendered miserable by refinement and mystery, we will think and declare our thoughts, not as Politicians, but as *Men*, as *Citizens*, and as *Volunteers!*

As MEN, therefore, we think, that Government is a trust for the use of the People—the PEOPLE, in the largest sense of that misapprehended word. We think that the Public Weal is the end of Government, and the forms of Government are merely the mutable means for obtaining this end; means that may be modelled or changed by the real will of the Public; a will supreme;—paramount to all other authority.

* *Sic* in original.

As Citizens, we think, that no people can promise unconditional obedience; and that obedience itself ceases to be a duty, when the will of the people ceases to be the law of the land.

As Volunteers, we think, that the Force of the People should form the guarantee of Freedom; and that their freedom is the only sure guarantee of Public Happiness.

Here, then, we take our stand,—and, if we be asked, what is the French Revolution to us? we answer—Much.

First, Much as Men. It is good for human nature that the grass grows where the Bastille stood. We do rejoice at an event which seemed the breaking of a charm that held *universal* France in a Bastille of civil and religious bondage. When we behold this enormous and misshapen Pile of Abuses, cemented merely by custom, and raised upon the ignorance of a prostrate People, tottering to its base—to the very level of equal liberty and common weal, we do really rejoice at this Resurrection of Human Nature; and we congratulate our Brother Man, coming forth from the Vaults of ingenious Torture, and from the Cave of Death. We do congratulate the Christian World that there is in it one great Nation, that has renounced all ideas of conquest, and has published the first glorious Manifesto of Humanity, of Union, and of Peace. In return, we pray to God that Peace may rest in their Land; and that it may never be in the power of Royalty, Nobility, or a *Priesthood*, to disturb the harmony of a people, consulting about those Laws which must ensure their own Happiness, and that of unborn Millions. The French Revolution is therefore much to us as Men, and much to us,

Secondly, as Irishmen. We too have a Country, and we hold it very dear—so dear to us its *Interest*, that we wish all *civil and religious intolerance* annihilated in this land—so dear to us its *Honour*, that we wish an eternal stop to the Traffic of Public Liberty which is bought by one and sold to another—so dear to us its *Freedom*, that we wish for nothing so much as *a real representative of the national will*, the surest guide and guardian of national happiness.

Go on then—Great and Gallant People!—to practice the sublime philosophy of your legislation; to force applause from nations least disposed to do you justice; and not by conquest, but by the omnipotence of reason, to convert and liberate the *world*—a World whose eyes are fixed on you; whose heart is with you; who talks of you with all their tongues. You are, in very truth, the Hope of this World; of all except a few men in a few Cabinets, who thought the human race belonged to them, not they to the human race; but now are taught by awful example, and tremble; and dare not confide in armies arrayed against you and your cause.

Resolved unanimously, That a Copy of this Declaration be forthwith transmitted, in our Name, by our President, to the National Assembly of France.

WILLIAM SHARMAN, President.

At a Select Meeting of the Friends of Universal Peace and Liberty, held at the Thatched-house Tavern,
London, August 20, 1791,

The following Address and Declaration to our Fellow Citizens was agreed on, and ordered to be published.

Friends and Fellow Citizens,

AT a moment like the present, when wilful misrepresentations are industriously spread by the Partizans of Arbitrary Power, and the Advocates of Passive Obedience and Court Government, we think it incumbent on us to declare to the world our Principles, and the Motives of our Conduct.

We rejoice at the glorious event of the *French Revolution.*

If it be asked—What is the French Revolution to us?

We answer (as has already been answered in another place), *It is much*—much to us as Men—much to us as Englishmen.

As Men, we rejoice in the Freedom of Twenty-five Millions of our Fellow-men. We rejoice in the prospect which such a magnificent example opens to the world. We congratulate the French Nation for having laid the axe to the root of Tyranny, and for erecting Government on the *Sacred Hereditary Rights of Man*—Rights which appertain to ALL, and not to *any* ONE more than to another. We know of no human authority superior to that of a whole Nation; and we profess and proclaim it as our principle, that every Nation has, at all times, an inherent indefeasible right to constitute and establish such Government for itself as best accords with its disposition, interest, and happiness.

As Englishmen, we also rejoice, because we are *immediately* interested in the French Revolution.

Without enquiring into the justice on either side, of the reproachful charges of intrigue and ambition, which the English and French Courts have constantly made on each other!—We confine ourselves to this observation:

That if the Court of France *only* was in fault, and the numerous Wars which have distressed both countries, are chargeable on her *alone,* that Court now exists no longer; and the cause and the consequence must cease together. The French, therefore, by the Revolution they have made, have conquered for us, as well as for themselves; if it be true, that *their* Court only was in fault, and ours never.—On this state of the case the French Revolution concerns us *immediately.*

We are oppressed with a heavy national debt, a burthen of taxes, and an expensive Administration of Government, beyond those of any people in the world.

We have also a very numerous Poor; and we hold that the moral obligation of providing for Old Age, helpless Infancy, and Poverty, is far superior to that of supplying the invented wants of Courtly Extravagance, Ambition, and Intrigue.

We believe there is no instance to be produced, but in England, of *Seven* Millions of Inhabitants, which make but little more than *One* Million of Families, paying yearly *Seventeen* Millions of Taxes.

As it has always been held out by all Administrations, that the restless ambition of the Court of France, rendered this expence necessary to us for our own defence, we consequently rejoice as Men deeply interested in the French Revolution (for that Court, as we have already said, exists no longer) and consequently the same enormous expences need not continue to us.

Thus rejoicing, as we sincerely do, both as Men, and Englishmen, as Lovers of universal Peace and Freedom, and as Friends to our own national prosperity, and a reduction of our public expences:— We cannot but express our astonishment, that any part or any Members of our own Government, should reprobate the extinction of that very Power in France, or wish to see it restored, to whose influence they formerly attributed (whilst they appeared to lament) the enormous increase of our own burthens and taxes.

What then, Are they sorry that the pretence for new oppressive taxes, and the occasion for continuing many old taxes, will be at an end!—If so, and if it is the policy of Courts and Court-government to prefer enemies to friends, and a system of war to that of peace, as affording more pretences for Places, Offices, Pensions, Revenue, and Taxation, it is high time for the people of every nation to look with circumspection to their own interests.

Those who *pay* the expence, and *not* those who *participate* in the emoluments arising from it, are the persons immediately interested in enquiries of this kind. We are a part of that national body, on whom the annual expence of Seventeen Millions falls; and we consider the present opportunity of the French Revolution, as a most happy one for lessening the enormous load under which this nation groans. If this be not done, we shall then have reason to conclude, that the cry of intrigue and ambition against *other* Courts, is no more than the common Cant of *all* Courts.

We think it also necessary to express our astonishment that a government desirous of being *called* FREE, should *prefer* connexions with the most despotic and arbitrary powers in Europe. We know of none more deserving this description than those of Turkey and Prussia, and the whole combination of German despots. Separated as we happily are by nature from the tumults of the Continent, we reprobate all systems and intrigues which sacrifice (and that too at a great expence) the blessings of our natural situation—Such systems cannot have a national origin.

If we are asked, what Government is? We hold it to be nothing more than a NATIONAL ASSOCIATION; and we hold that to be the best,

which

which secures to every man his rights, and promotes the greatest quantity of happiness with the *least expence*. We live to improve, or we live in vain; and therefore we admit of no maxims of government or policy, on the mere score of antiquity or other men's authority, the *old* whigs or the *new*. We will exercise the reason with which we are endued, or we possess it unworthily. As reason is given at all times, it is for the purpose of being used at all times.

Among the blessings which the French Revolution has produced to that nation, we enumerate the abolition of the Feudal system of injustice and tyranny, on the 4th of August, 1789.

Beneath the Feudal system all Europe has long groaned; and from it England is not yet free. Game Laws, Borough Tenures, and tyrannical monopolies of numerous kinds still remain amongst us. But rejoicing, as we sincerely do, in the freedom of others, till we shall happily accomplish our own, we intended to commemorate this prelude to the universal extirpation of the Feudal system, by meeting on the anniversary of that day (the 4th of August) at the Crown and Anchor. From this meeting we were prevented by the interference of certain *unnamed* and *skulking* persons with the master of the tavern, who informed us, that on *their* representations he could not receive us.———Let those who live by, or countenance Feudal oppressions, take the reproach of this ineffectual meanness and cowardice to themselves. They cannot stifle the public declaration of our honest, open, and avowed opinions.

These are our principles, and these our sentiments.

They embrace the interest and happiness of the great body of the nation, of which we are a part. As to Riots and Tumults, let those answer for them who by wilful misrepresentations, endeavour to excite and promote them; or, who seek to *stun* the sense of the nation, and lose the great cause of public good, in the outrages of a misinformed mob. We take our ground on principles that require no such riotous aid. We have nothing to apprehend from the poor; for we are pleading their cause. And we fear not proud oppression, for we have Truth on our side. We say, and we repeat it, that the French Revolution opens to the world an opportunity in which all good citizens must rejoice, that of promoting the general happiness of Man. And that it, moreover, offers to this Country in particular, an opportunity of reducing our enormous Taxes.

These are our objects, and we will pursue them.

J. HORNE TOOKE, Chairman.

FINIS.

Printed by *Corns* and *Bartlect*, *High Street* and *Union Street*, *Birmingham*.

www.ingramcontent.com/pod-product-compliance
Lightning Source LLC
Chambersburg PA
CBHW020337090426
42735CB00009B/1579